Praise for Jane P. Perry's WH

"From her own pages to the record of Samuel Pepys and many people in between, Jane P. Perry's *White Snake Diary* creates a collage that proves the enduring power of a diary to illuminate, educate, and amaze. Prepare yourself to become immersed and enchanted."

—Paula Tarnapol Whitacre, author of *A Civil Life in an Uncivil Time: Julia Wilbur's Struggle for Purpose*

"Jane P. Perry's *White Snake Diary* is compelling and important. Perry has written a lyrical and thought-provoking memoir that is also a meditation on memory-what we recall and how we record it."

—Susan G. Solomon, Curatorial Resources and Research, and author of *The Science of Play: How to Build Playgrounds that Enhance Children's Development*

"What is a "diary"? Is it strictly factual or can it reel into fancy? Does it record a life in words only or can it embrace images, even collages of personal event? Jane P. Perry's *White Snake Diary* both researches and ruminates on the diary as a multifaceted form, bending this way and that in response to historical as well as personal demands. At the same time, Perry (re)enacts her own diaristic play, beginning with her nine-year-old self up through the present day, summoning an interplay of voices that snake across years and intensifying emotional terrain. *White Snake*'s commentary on dream, family, and the complexity of memory creates a beautiful, compelling artifact of author as "self-inscriber.""

—Merle L. Bachman, author of *Blood Party*

White Snake Diary:

Exploring
Self-Inscribers

By
Jane P. Perry

atmosphere press

Published by Atmosphere Press

Author photo by Kristin Cofer

Cover design by Nick Courtright

White Snake Diary
2020, Jane P. Perry

atmospherepress.com

To my mother Anne Therese Gorman Perry

The bees came out of the junipers, two small swarms
The size of melons; and golden, too, like melons,
They hung next to each other, at the height of a deer's breast
Above the wet black compost. And because
The light was very bright it was hard to see them,
And harder still to see what hung between them.
A snake hung between them.

from Brigit Pegeen Kelly's "The Dragon"

CONTENTS

PART I:
WHITE SNAKE SLEEPING

I

I wake up to crisp, clean, white sheets. Sun shines bright through the window. My husband sleeps at my left side. To my absolute horror, a humongous boa-sized white snake sleeps warm against my right side. My index finger is in the snake's mouth, lodged there by a fang. The fang punctures the tip of my finger. I feel no pain.

I think. If I just keep quiet and do not move, stifling my rapid heartbeat, I will be safe. What I do, however, is slowly and meticulously slip my finger off of its mooring. I am exceedingly grateful that the snake is so lethargic. Its somnambulistic, dead weight tells me I am not in immediate danger.

I wake my husband to alert him. We have to be at an appointment. If we let this sleeping snake lie, only to return to an empty bed, we will be wracked with anxiety. Shall we stuff the snake in a pillow case? Bundle and tie it up in the sheet? Then what will we do with it? Our appointment looms. I abandon this frantic predicament and wake up.

* * *

What has just visited me? While I could riff on the obvious associations of predation generally and sexual predation specifically, I can't shake the feeling that alongside a remnant of what is horrifying in the dream is also a deep reassuring force. I did stealthily extract myself. The horror dissolved into a problematic annoyance.

Snakes are represented across cultures and religions, in mythology and folklore. They are found in our most ancient art. The evolutionary anthropologist Lynne A. Isbell argues in *The Fruit, the Tree, and the Serpent: Why We See So Well* that recent neurobiological evidence shows the predation pressure from snakes is responsible for our superior vision and large brains.[1] The snake is a symbol in medicine, healing, fertility, wisdom, danger, and rejuvenation.[2] After sloughing its skin, a white snake can signify re-emergence, rebirth, and transformation. I record this dream as the first entry of a new diary because it is so vivid, when most of my nighttime neural meanderings nowadays either vanish just after waking or cunningly hide from notice altogether. This diary will help me explore the message the white snake has for me. Not surprisingly, we will start in the garden.

---

[1] Isbell, Lynne A. *The Fruit, the Tree, and the Serpent: Why We See So Well.* Harvard University Press, 2009.

[2] Noble, Vicki, editor. *Uncoiling the Snake: Ancient Patterns in Contemporary Women's Lives.* Harper, 1993.

PART II:
MY GARDEN STORY

What is a diary, and why do we keep them? Merriam-Webster defines "diary" as "a record of events, transactions, or observations kept daily or at frequent intervals; a record of personal activities, reflections, or feelings."[3] Sounds simple enough. Certainly a diary can be institutional in nature, a bookkeeper's prim record of transactions and accounts. But a diary can also surrender to the unconscious, vault free of restrictions, incorporate just about any idea or object. A diary need not be restricted to words. Some diary-keepers use a collage form to create "a kind of surrealist art in which bits of flat objects, as newspaper, cloth, pressed flowers, etc., are pasted together in incongruous relationship for their symbolic or suggestive effect."[4] Nor need one's diary be written on paper. Cave paintings, clay tablets, rock carvings, papyrus, videos, blogs—all have been used to record hopes, desires, ideas, records, incantations.

Why do we do it? Why do we feel the need to journal? Why does one feel compelled to record one's life, to collect memories and reflections? What makes

---

[3] *Webster's New Twentieth Century Dictionary of the English Language, Unabridged*, second edition, The Publishers Guild, 1955.

[4] Ibid.

the cut? What is too mundane—or too unspeakable—to include? What does the diary as a literary genre look like and what can it tell us?

I am in a junk store that calls itself a "depot for creative reuse." It is fertile ground, rich with the germinating possibilities of baskets of ribbons, bins of greeting cards, a box of surplus glass vials, another of bottle caps, reams of perforated computer paper, empty envelopes, half used wrapping paper, books, tired and incomplete board games, cardboard tubes, swatches of hot pink tulle, corks, and drawers and drawers of pens. I rummage through stacks of empty photo albums. Among them, I come across one that is not empty. It contains a snapshot chronology of a smiling girl I will call Caroline. Crisp notes are jotted on the reverse: "Caroline's school play," "7 years old," "Caroline with her Easter basket," "Caroline singing with her class," "Caroline and her glove—on graduation day!" "January 2004." This photo collection is my garden bouquet, a palette evoking familiar childhood landmarks.

I head toward the cashier, carrying the empty albums I wanted, and the Caroline photos I discovered. On a nearby side table, next to a threadbare overstuffed chair with elaborate mahogany-carved armrests, I spy a child's diary. I have the same diary, in blue, saved from when I was young. I leave the diary. But I look for my own blue diary when I return home.

I am drawn to Caroline's snapshots, which spark memories from my own childhood. I add to my new diary, weaving into it bits of these memories. With Caroline by my side, I insert school assignments, snapshot-inspired vignettes, childhood diary entries, cereal box text, poems, letters, doodles, dreams. At times I wonder whether I'm creating my own diary or Caroline's. I continue on into my present life, with workplace documents, essays, telephone conversations and professional reports. Caroline's role is over, I tell myself. She was a muse for my new diary. I thank her for her help, and plan to dismiss her, proceeding with my own stories, inspired by her snapshots. But something in the energy of her photos insists on my attention. Caroline wants to come along for the ride.[5]

---

[5] The photos of Caroline have been altered for confidentiality.

2

3

The plush, white cotton turtleneck shirts arrive in one size so everyone in Caroline's class will fit into them. Once on, Marcel finds he can make a comfortable tent by tucking both knees under his shirt and mooring his feet to the bottom seam. Rita has an extra quarter-sleeve's worth of material lodged at both wrists, blocked by the extra thick cuff. This keeps her warm when the back door to the auditorium is propped open.

Caroline stands between Marcel and Rita. With both hands at her sides, Caroline holds out the bottom of her shirt so that it flares just slightly. She likes the soft feeling between her fingers. She breathes gently and looks straight ahead. Marcel looks to his right, talking. Rita watches the teacher, who has moved to hoist the curtain.

4

My Garden Story, A true story
By Caroline
Marcel and I crust the drt
into little pesis over the bulbs
an then we dusted our hand
an then we wr to recess.

* * *

When it comes to nature diaries, a just-the-facts approach can be fascinating. Darwin's research notations on geology, animals, and fossils while exploring the South American coast via the ship H.M.S. Beagle from 1832 through 1836 provide clues to his subsequent theory of evolution.[6] Such precise records can reveal the wonders around us that usually go unnoticed.

In *Baby Birds: An Artist Looks into the Nest,* ornithologist and natural history illustrator Julie Zickefoose records the daily developmental

---

[6] Bell, Thomas, et al. *The Zoology of the voyage of H.M.S. Beagle, under the command of Captain Fitzroy, R.N., during the years 1832 to 1836: Published with the approval of the Lords Commissioners of Her Majesty's Treasury.* London: Published by Smith, Elder and Co..., to 1843, 1839. Pdf. Retrieved from the Library of Congress, <www.loc.gov/item/06016152/>. Accessed 19 November 2019.

progression of birds from hatchling to fledgling, which had never been done before.[7] Zickefoose lays the nestling on a bed of tissues directly on her diary page for an as-close-to-exact watercolor rendering in life-size, notations included, before the hatchling exhibits readiness to return to the nest. In thirteen years, she has studied the eastern bluebird, tree swallow, Carolina chickadee, ruby-throated hummingbird, chimney swift, tufted titmouse, house wren, house sparrow, and European starling, to name a few.

[7] Zickefoose, Julie. *Baby Birds: An Artist Looks into the Nest.* Houghton Mifflin Harcourt, 2016.

5

To make the night go faster, I put myself to bed early. I arrange my stuffed animals around me, making sure they all receive the same number of kisses. Inadvertently launching a barrage of affection on Fluffy the dog, I methodically return to cast a balance of kisses to the other animals. I brush Fluffy's white curls. I love Fluffy so much. I love Nana so much. I love Mommy and Daddy so much. I feel how sad I would be were Nana to die. What about if Mommy died? Or Daddy? Tears begin to flow. I lie down, wet-faced, and with my animals around me, fall asleep.

6

On the morning of my ninth birthday, I receive a gold-embossed, blue leather pocket-sized Five Year Diary. Inside the diary, there is a page for each day of the year. Every page is divided into five rows with four lines allotted to each year. Under "THE PROPERTY OF" I write my name.

Outside, clouds open to a downpour that floods the driveway. Each raindrop, so full of water, makes a hemispherical bubble that rides the water-layered asphalt for several seconds so that at any given moment a mottled, domed surface punctuates the pavement. Bubbles pop and new bubbles form as the rain continues to fall. All at once, the water surface settles. A wisp of a breeze flutters in a lisp across the drench.

7

Feel icky. Had to go to the Metical Center to be cultured. Wore my p.j.s

Temp. today first 103, then 100.4. Yesterday temp. was 102.4. Sore throat bothers me a lot. So far I've been out of school 4 days.

Had a piano lesson today. I got a seal! Seal means good, good, good, good! I also had dancing.

Went to a dog show after church. Saw a lot of (toy collies?) and <u>many</u> poodles. One time the dogs would have to sit for 3 or 4 min. while their owners went into another room.

Went to Nana's House. Had some of our cake and some of her cocoa. Cousins came and played some of their games. Was fun!

At school today I had to have my hearing checked again. I couldn't hear anything. Then the nurse try to hear. She couldn't. Said it was broken. Whew!

8

I wake in the morning surprised and bewildered to discover I am wearing different pajamas than the ones I put on the previous evening. As I dress for school, I try to remember what pajamas I wore to bed.

Daddy has gone to work. Mommy has laid out my vitamin and fluoride pill next to my juice glass, already filled.

9

Caroline fills her empty bowl with Mr. T Cereal Fortified with B-Vitamins and Iron. She pours milk over the cereal as she reads from the back of the box. "Hey kids, start your day the Mr. T way!" Mr. T is surrounded by two kids about Caroline's age and their mother. Below this gathering is a series of cartoon frames.

The mother and two kids stand expectantly next to a parked truck with Mr. T boldly printed on the side of the cab. "Here it comes!" says Mother. "Great!" says the daughter. "I can hardly—Hey, wait!"

"Come back!" exclaims the son.

Mr. T arrives. "What's a matter kids?"

In unison the family replies "Mr. T! Somebody just drove away with our Mr. T cereal!"

With Mr. T in the foreground and the family running close behind, the son's hand waving, Mr. T calls out, "They won't get away with it! Come on!"

Caroline crunches her cereal with punctuated satisfaction while the sweetened, cool milk slips around the inside of her mouth.

Mr. T, giant-sized, peers through a window. "That's them all right. I know how to handle them!" The family, behind Mr. T and in silhouette, screech "EEEEE" in bold red.

The family's screech magnifies. The robbers, surprised mid-bite by the window-framed Mr. T, establish a plan: "It's the cops. Run for it!"

Muscles bulging, Mr. T grabs both robbers, one of whom shows a red heart tattoo inscribed with MOM.

The family surrounds Mr. T. "Thanks for your help and thanks for the delicious new Mr. T cereal!"

10

Forest Life
Jane Perry
4th Grade

It was a lovely day. The clouds sailed through the sky just like creampuffs. The air was filled with the smell of pine. Deep in the forest there were two baby robins and their mother. Their mother was saying, "I'm not going to be with you all the time." Then Norma spoke up, "Why?" "Because you won't be a baby anymore." "Why?" "Because you will be growing up." "Why?" Her mother was silent. "Mother." Janet said, "Will we ever see you again?" "Maybe," her mother said. It was getting dark. Janet and Norma were getting tired. "Time for bed." They snuggled up close to their mother and fell fast asleep. "You'll make a fine women," she said softly.

* * *

Zickefoose caused a stir amongst those brought up believing that human scent will turn a mother away from her babies. On the contrary, the mother bird tolerated Zickefoose's daily interruption. One wonders if Zickefoose feeding the nestling mashed mealworm (and recording in exact pictorial detail the resulting fecal sac) was also a very good deal for the mother bird, temporarily giving her one less mouth to feed.

After his two years out on Walden Pond, the environmentalist Henry David Thoreau came back into town and, between stints as a surveyor and lecturer, devoted the rest of his life to a fastidious documentation of the flora and fauna of Concord, Massachusetts. He entered field notes on scraps of paper. He collected specimens in a sewn-in compartment of his "botany hat."[8] He sketched. He pressed wildflowers between diary pages. Andrea Wulf, writing in *The Atlantic* in 2017, reports on his compulsive meticulousness: He used his walking stick to take measurements. In the evenings and mornings, he tabulated his measurements and wrote long stream-of-consciousness entries, reporting not only his every incident and move but his awe-embracing love and joy in the wonders of nature. He tasted lichen. He logged the number of bubbles trapped under ice. He reported bird songs, cricket chirps and the loping of a fox.[9] He sketched an indigenous willow fishtrap, then, years later wrote

---

[8] Walls, Laura Dassow. *Henry David Thoreau: A Life*. University of Chicago Press, 2017, p. 330.

[9] Wulf, Andrea. "*Walden* Wasn't Thoreau's Masterpiece," *The Atlantic*, November 2017, www.theatlantic.com/magazine/archive/2017/11/what-thoreau-saw/540615/. Accessed 8 November 2018.

about the humbling lessons of this craft learned from the Abenaki. [10]

Thoreau started his diary in October 1837 as a young man just out of college, and kept it to November 1861, when he was too weak to write. He would die six months later. Totaling forty-seven manuscript volumes, some of Thoreau's journals can be viewed online through the Thoreau Library at the University of California, Santa Barbara.[11] One hundred and fifty years after Thoreau's authorship, Boston University biology professor Richard Primack and National Park Service researcher Abraham Miller-Rushing used Thoreau's prodigious catalogue of leafing dates to document climate change.[12]

A compulsion to record our experience is the effort to find answers and make order out of apparent chaos.

---

[10] Walls, Laura Dassow. *Henry David Thoreau: A Life.* University of Chicago Press, 2017.

[11] "Online Journal Transcripts." *The Writings of Henry D. Thoreau.* University of California, Santa Barbara, thoreau.library.ucsb.edu/writings_journals.html. Accessed 5 September 2018.

[12] Primack, Richard B. and Abraham J. Miller-Rushing, "Uncovering, Collecting, and Analyzing Records to Investigate the Ecological Impacts of Climate Change: A Template from Thoreau's Concord." *BioScience,* vol. 62. no.2, 2012, pp.170–181, academic.oup.com/bioscience/article/62/2/170/280145. Accessed 16 September, 2018.

II

<u>foil balls</u>
<u>float or sink?</u>
By Caroline Carter
2nd Grade

<u>Instructions</u>: Take a foil square and crumple it up so it floats. Take a foil square and carmple it up so it sinks.

<u>Hypothesis</u>: I wanted to see what happened when I dropped my foil ball in the water. I thought it might float.

<u>Background Information</u>: Aluminum is a silvery chemical. It is very light. It doesn't weigh much. It is easy to made into a shape. When it is made into foil it is easy to rip. Aluminum foil is used for kooking and saving. It is used to make tape and bags. The Croydon Ball is a famous aluminum ball in England. It is made of KitKat wrappers. It weighs 1572 kg. That is 3458 ½ pounds. It has air trapped inside.

<u>Procedure</u>: One day I got in the bath and I had a foil ball. And I dropped it in the water. And it floated. Then I ran into the kitchin. I got another piece of aluminum foil. I got back into the bath. I crumpled it up under the water. I wanted to see what happened. The crumpled up foil sank! Then I told Daddy I discovered something.

<u>Conclusion</u>: Here is what I discovered. A foil ball crumpled in air floats. This is because air is trapped and air is lighter than water. A foil ball crumpled in water

sinks. The water trapped in the foil balls weighs the same as the water not trapped. So the weight of the foil makes it sink.

12

I sit erect at my desk because I have found that the clarity of my telephone line is somehow related to my posture. "I love you, Mom . . . Hi, Mom. . . It's your daughter, Mom . . . It is your daughter, Jane." I am not in any rush, by my own admission to the receptionist who corralled several staff people to achieve this opportunity. "I love you so much, Mom."

And then, there is the uptake: "I love you all the time!"

This makes me laugh. "I know! I love you all the time." I sing, "I love you in the morning and in the afternoon. I love you in the evening and underneath the moon. I love you." I sing because I have read that the auditory portion of the brain is one of the last to disengage.

"I don't like this office," Mom offers.

"The people who answered the phone thought it would be a good idea for you and I to talk in an office," I say while simultaneously chastising myself for being too wordy.

"I love you," I say into the silence. "I love you." I wait. I sing some more.

"I see boxes under my chair," Mom shares.

"Boxes?"

"What?"

Orient, I instruct myself. "You are in an office."

"I am so tired," Mom laments.

"I know you are," I comfort. "Would you like to nap?"

Silence.

"I am going to look on the desk to see what is next to do."

Oh no! Not the desktop! What is the staff thinking? But I reflect back, "You have worked at many desks, Mom."

"We should not talk long," Mom says.

"Would you like to hang up?"

"Wait."

Silence. Then a muffled drop of weight, what I imagine from her grunt is Mom sitting back down. "I talked to your sister."

Oh! This is fun, I think, because I do not have a sister. "How's she doing?"

"She is fine!"

"Great! Glad to hear it." I do not ask for details. Requests for retrieval stun my mother into silence. Today Mom is silent anyway.

"I love you, Mom."

"I love you, too. We should not talk anymore."

I like that Mom feels initiative by telling me what to do. "OK. I will call you again. OK?"

"I am going to hang up."

"I love you."

"Bye."

"Bye."

13

Plants with soft flexible stems usally live for only one growing season. Plants with thick, stiff stems usally live for many years.

taproot—the main part of a root that goes deep into the soil. small hairs that come off the main root take in nutrient.

fibrous roots—many roots the same size which grow long, but, not deep

In root growth, cells from the root cap are shed and returned to the soil.

14

Tonight Mrs. Long saw a saucer shaped thing flying in the air. She said it had white and green lights blinking. It went right over our neighborhood! The radio put callers in by people who saw this thing. They think it might be a meataor. I'm a little scared.

Had softball game. The score ended up 1 to 1, after 2 innings, I think. I didn't get to bat, so next time the people who didn't bat are up first.

Had a substitute for reading. Had to miss the softball game for the second time. It's 8:30, I don't like Mommy.

Played with Rita again. Whent to her house to play school. Like Rita, but sort of get sick of playing school all the time at her house.

Stayed at school till 4:00 to practice chorus. Fun! But didn't get my hair washed as planned.

I HATE MOM! DAD TOO. I asked her if I could watch T.V. and she yelled at me. Then Dad yelled at me. Now I have to miss my show. I love Mom. She just made up. Now I can watch T.V.

15

The monuments loom massively as Caroline struggles in her imagination: millions of ant-like carriers, roped to pulleys dragging stone block after stone block, carving huge dents in the plains for hundreds of miles—much longer than her bus ride. Or were these humungous stones aerially hoisted and then stacked crosswise by aliens from another planet, who then visited neighborhoods thousands of years later? Caroline stands erect in her green jacket, feet together and sneakers so white and unblemished as to distract from the Sarsen stones behind her.

16

Plants Dead or Alive
Caroline Carter
4th Grade

Purpose: To find out if rock and roll kills a plant.

Hypothesis: My science project is to prove that music from Live 105 (rock and roll and heavy metal) will kill a plant.

Procedure:

1. First I went to Longs Drugs and bought two plants that were healthy and the same plant.

2. I put one plant in my bedroom window facing south (experiment). I put the second plant in the kitchen window facing south (control).

3. I watered the plants and measured them.

4. For four days I turned my radio on to Live 105.3 closed my bedroom door and left for school.

5. When I got home I turned off the music and objerved and measured it, and took notes.

6. After a week of watering and keeping them by the window I compared my two plants.

Background Information: Heavy metal rock from Live 105 will impede the normal growth and development of plants. But, loud classical music, like William tell Overture helps growth and development of plants (from "The Effect of Music on Plants"). My plant is listening to heavy metal and rock. At first it was fine but then the music started to impede the growth and development of the plant.

<u>Conclusion</u>: On the first day of the science fair project I played the music for my plant the lenth of the school day. The first day my plant was fine, and also for two more days but on the third day it started to die and for the next two day it was still dieing. My control plant (no music) is still fresh and living with the same water and sun as my experiment.

Notes

Date	control plant	experiment plant
May 18th	two blossongs coming	two blossongs not
after music	One dead one coming	one same
May 19th	One came up to make	One dead to make 1.
May	two. 5½ in. tall	5½ in. tall
May 20th	same	same
May 21st	two blossongs	two dieing and one blossong living.
May 22th	same	same
May 23rd	Same but 4 blossong coming. 6 in	1 blossong came to make two 6 in
May 24th	Same	blossong drooping and leaves drooping
May 25th	same. 6 in.	same. 6 in.

35

17

My cousins Harry, Andy and I are upstairs in my room playing Mad Libs, sending us into fits of laughter, which quickly morph into mock kicking into the bed pillows and much tossing of stuffed animals. I howl in laughter. Andy starts throwing animals at Harry. Harry starts bucking and hooting. "Wait. Wait. Let me finish," I try. "Needless to say, havoc ensues as the lions continue to—"

"Poop!" Harry finishes while Andy and I dissolve into gasping laughter. Harry grabs the book. "Needless to say, havoc ends as the lions continue to poop everything in sight! Ahhhhh!" I grab for the Mad Libs. Harry deflects and whips a stuffed animal at me. Andy tackles me. I lift Andy and throw him on Harry. Andy bounces off Harry and falls off the bed with a reverberating thud. We three immediately freeze. Harry yells "poop!" I wing a pillow at Harry. Andy jumps up, yells "dookey!" and launches himself onto both Harry and I, just as Daddy storms into the room.

"Jane!" Daddy yells. "Go comb your hair!"

The room is silent. I extract myself from Harry, Andy, a pillow, and three stuffed animals, and haul myself off the bed. I exit to the bathroom. Heart beating fast from the wrestling match, Daddy's reprimand bounces in matched rhythm. I look in the mirror and swallow dryly.

The writer of a diary must be disciplined. I kept a headache diary when I was working full time, with young children and a marriage, as if the cause wasn't obvious enough. Some diarists carefully and methodically record actions, incidents and amounts, for example, in a food journal, a sleep diary, a travel log or a war diary. Historically, diarists had the benefit of education and economic means, including time, to accumulate records, making the Latin derivative of diary, "daily allowance," all the more poignant. Diary writing, whether for accounting or personal reflection, is not for the faint of heart, as Louis Menand noted in a *New Yorker* piece in 2007: "The impulse to keep a diary is to actual diaries as the impulse to go on a diet is to actual slimness."[13] We may think our lives are meaningful in commentary, or that the purposeful habit itself is of value, but the very routine can begin to feel repetitive as is often the case with the regular passage of time. Nonetheless, we have inscribers in our midst, and, thanks to editors, translators, and searchers of ephemera who discover, decipher, notate obtuse

---

[13] Menand, Louis. "Woke Up This Morning: Why Do We Read Diaries?" *The New Yorker*, December 10, 2007, www.newyorker.com/magazine/2007/12/10/woke-up-this-morning. Accessed 15 August 2018.

references and otherwise render such records available, the public benefits.

Some diarists offer thrilling, eye-witness accounts of disasters and celebrations. Through them we can move beyond the events and into the human experience. We gain historical color and invaluable insight. Emilie Davis, a young, free African American woman in Philadelphia during the time of the Civil War, recorded the flight of residents from Gettysburg to Philadelphia during the Battle of Gettysburg, the fall of Vicksburg, and the funeral procession of Abraham Lincoln.[14] She was there. She tells us what she saw. The United States Holocaust Memorial Museum in Washington, D.C. features oral histories, memories and diaries that chronicle 20th century Nazi persecution, deportation, resistance, and death of loved ones, as well as the everyday scrounging for food and playing of games.[15]

---

[14] Davis, Emilie. *The Emilie Davis Diaries*. Eberly Family Special Collections Library,
Penn State University Libraries,
libraries.psu.edu/about/collections/emilie-davis-diaries. Accessed 5 September 2018.

[15] "Diaries." The United States Holocaust Memorial Museum, www.ushmm.org/collections/bibliography/diaries. Accessed 19 November 19, 2019.

18

Mommy kisses me awake. The television is on. I do not pay attention to the opening cartoons of the show. I wait for Captain Bob, with his snappy sea shanty cap and scruffy beard, so different from Daddy's clean-shaven face. Suddenly there he is saying, "Today is Jane's seventh birthday! Happy birthday, Jane!"

A photo of me, smiling, fills the screen. I know that dress. I know that girl with the carefully combed hair. "Jane, your present is," and Captain Bob hesitates for effect, "behind the couch!"

I shriek. I dive for the back of the sofa, perching on my hips. There is a present behind the couch! I retrieve the lumpy package. Nothing. Nothing. Ever. Will match this moment in thrill.

19

Inside the paper wrapping is Belle, a doll. Belle accompanies Caroline to the breakfast table. Sitting tucked into the crook of Caroline's arm, Belle and Caroline share the same pulled-back-from-the-face black hair. Belle's part is more prominent. Belle's netted frock scratches the inside of Caroline's left elbow, but Caroline pretends not to mind because that is what a loving mother does.

Caroline eats her breakfast with one hand. She drinks milk from her snowman glass. Caroline smiles in the love of her mother's eyes upon her. Two faces reflect off the highly varnished table surface.

20

Caroline eyes her flutophone. White scraped indents from previous children mar the recorder's red plastic mouthpiece. Caroline cradles a cherry pit in her mouth as she awaits the final moments before the second-grade performance. She spins the small stone with her tongue, pleased with its smooth, clean surface. She lodges the pit between her upper and lower molars, pushing down hard, then slipping it into her cheek.

Caroline looks out to the audience, as does Marcel. Caroline knows she can play with the cherry pit in her mouth even though she has never done this before. Caroline likes this stone and she likes that she is keeping it on stage.

Caroline plays with Marcel, Rita, and the other classmates against the light of an electric candle flickering on a school desk stage-left. When the two class songs end and the clapping dies down, Caroline turns to Rita and smiles. The cherry pit is balanced on the edges of her front teeth.

21

The Yo-Yo
Jane Perry
3rd Grade

The yo-yo is believed to be the oldest toy. It was invented thousands of years ago in China. Some drawing of a yo-yo were found in Eqyptian temples.

The yo-yo wasn't a toy, it was played with by adults. King Louis XVII played with a yo-yo. Soldiers, generals, and even opera characters played with them.

In 1866, the yo-yo came to United States. Donald Duncan started a company and gave the yo-yo its name. He sold them to children by having contests and demonstrations, and by 1962 he had sold 45 million yo-yos.

22

My birthday party! Rita gave me some pencils that can be used for paints, Lily, a necklace, also got a wallat, a 2 headed troll, jump rope, jacks, Badminton, a tennis racket and Balls, and China Dogs.

* * *

The everyday details are indeed what can bring the past alive, filling the gaps that the big history books overlook. Fortunately, we have had an abundance of compulsive diarists who help us understand daily life in their eras. The noted English civil servant Samuel Pepys wrote a diary in shorthand (for which he provided a key).[16] His is an unfiltered account of turbulence, culture and domesticity of British life during the reign of Charles II and the second Dutch War, the Great Plague and the Great Fire of London and including everything from historical events to meetings with royalty, dancing as a means of upward mobility, infidelities, and frets over his wife's irregular menses.

---

[16] Rogers, Pat. "Pepys's Place." *London Review of Books.* vol. 5, no. 11, 16 June, 1983, www.lrb.co.uk/v05/n11/pat-rogers/pepyss-place. Accessed 23 September 2018.

He wrote from 1660 to 1669—until he stopped, thinking, mistakenly, that he was going blind.

The thirty-seven diaries of Thomas Thistlewood, a mid-eighteenth century Jamaican planter and slave-owner, detail the assignment of work and provisions, discipline, personal and sexual relationships—some with slaves—slave rebellions, and lists of temperature and rainfall amounts.[17]

A diary found on the frozen body of Robert Falcon Scott, an Antarctic explorer, gives a harrowing account of his two-year expedition in 1910, which ended in the death of his small team in a makeshift tent on the Great Ice Barrier. His diary ends with a plea to take care of the surviving families back home: "Last entry. For God's sake look after our people."[18]

Fast-forward to a string of Twitter entries under the hashtag #OldManDiary, posted by Snotgirl (@Fawn_Liebowitz). She publishes snapshots of diary pre-print pages. The man's terse handwritten accounting of the day's mundane events—"May 15, 87 1st day of swimming low 55 hi 75 . . . replace furniture wash off all

---

[17] "Thomas Thistlewood Papers." James Marshall and Marie-Louise Osborn Collection, Beinecke Rare Book and Manuscript Library. Yale University.
beinecke.library.yale.edu/collections/highlights/thomas-thistlewood-papers. Accessed 20 September 2018.

[18] Scott, Robert Falcon. "Captain Scott's diary, volume 3". British Library, www.bl.uk/collection-items/captain-scotts--diary. Accessed 23 September 2018.

deck and sidewalk water all garden spread grass between rows on beans . . . Willie Mays 7 home run Henry Aaron 15th home run"[19] — is strangely compulsive reading.

What makes for good reading in a diary? It's not always the momentous events that attract, but rather the simple activities that we share in our own lives and times. A twentieth century unpublished anonymous Michigan farm wife writes in sparse enumerations on the weather, household chores, correspondence, income and expenditures, and instances where interactions extend into social occasions —"They stayed until mid-nite. Had a nice evening."[20] We can see ourselves in the joys and letdowns. Sometimes it seems we are reading our own lives.

---

[19] @Fawn-Liebowitz. "Willie Mays 7 home run Henry Aaron 15th home run." *Twitter*, 24 May 2019, 8:37 a.m., twitter.com/Fawn_Liebowitz/status/1131947459310116864. Accessed 19 November, 2019.

[20] Bloom, Lynn Z. "'I Write for Myself and Strangers': Private Diaries as Public Documents." *Inscribing the Daily: Critical Essays on Women's Diaries,* edited by Suzanne L. Bunkers and Cynthia A. Huff, University of Massachusetts Press, 1996, p. 25.

23

EASTER! Nana came over for dinner. Had ham! Went to the Cousins. Stayed up till 9:00! Keen Day.

Dancing lessons today. Learned the bunny hop. Review old dances. Had a lot of homework. Got it all finished at 8:00!

Daddy stayed home today. He is in a <u>good</u> mood. I like him this way!

Had gym. Played baseball. I'm not so good. Used to be. After school played with Lily. Rita didn't want to but did anyway. She's dum.

Kind of took care of the Williams children today. Wasn't very fun, but sort of fun. Daddy and Mommy thanked me.

Went over to Rita's house. Can catch pretty good now. Started raining, and we played out in it!

Disagreable. I hate Daddy. Just because I was skipping down stairs he starts yelling at me. When ever he yells at me he always go down and tells Mommy.

Played with Lily. Found a four-leaf clover. Made me have no piano lesson! Marcel was sick now better because of clover!

SEPTEMBER 16

Fri 1966 Had filmstrip on Man. Also Played with everyone in the Kitty Cat Club. Talked about slumter partys. Stay out after supper till about 8:00!

24

I play a favorite game. I tunnel between the sheets of my tightly tucked bed. The deeper down I go, face-first, the faster my heart beats. I can still breathe but I feel like I can't. I press down further, heart racing, breathing, until there is no more room. This is just the end of the bed, I remind myself. With my face pushing hard into the hospital corners I breathe shallowly, feeling the fright. All at once I buck and kick to extract myself in reverse, each movement of retreat giving me more space around my face to breathe and a cumulative increase in relief until I am free and away from the pressing-in feeling and breathing and heart calming down.

25

Played outside after dinner with Rita.
Didn't go to bed til 9:45. Heard the 10:00
News.

Father's Day. Went to the beach with
our cousins. Got new tan slacks, tapered.
Had lemon morang pie. Dad forgot Noxema
for our sunburns so he got up out of T.V.
show just to get it for me. Kool guy.

Lily is nosey. She wanted to know why I
wasn't going to play with her today. Only 3
more days of school, not counting Sat. and
Sun. Only 18 more school hours to go!

26

The back wall of the stage announces in green construction paper GOING BUGGY. Netting cascades in moored dips where class-made bugs cling. Center net, an anthropomorphized, sassy-bellied insect smiles, its eyes a closed crescent. Perhaps to take the sting out of bug haters in the audience, this inflated mascot has red-dotted cheeks flanking its smile and perky black antennae.

Caroline's classmates sit, knees to chins, on two low risers on either side of the stage. Seated in the front row, Marcel is dressed all in black, hugging his black and white striped wing vertically to his tucked-in legs and torso. Shielded in winged casement, he looks attentively to Caroline, solo center stage. Lily also sits in the front row, two seats away from Marcel. She wears a sweater knit by her mother with crochet-knotted dots, black tights, and a long, fuchsia boa over both arms. In the back row, Rita wears a headdress of twenty-four-inch long, yellow foam petals that horseshoe around her face.

Caroline stands in a powder-green hooded sweatshirt and black tights. Stiff antennae sit on top of her hooded head. Translucent cellophane wings poke from either side of her shoulders. A beetle is visible through her left wing. Caroline rubs the hem of the sweatshirt. She smiles apologetically as she looks down, sharing a mutual humility with several of her classmates. These garden outfits, so fun to make at home and such a humbuzz nestled amongst each other backstage, suddenly feel awkward to these soon-to-be fifth graders as those soon to graduate watch from the audience below.

27

Caroline and Daddy stop along a wide garden path, empty aside from a threesome far ahead. The two appear small in the middle of the walkway amongst the trees in summer foliage. Caroline stands unbalanced, weight on her left foot. Dressed in a loose-fitting jersey and denim high-waisted shorts, she buries her right hand in the deep pocket. A bow keeps most of Caroline's bangs out of her eyes. Caroline thinks about Rita and wonders if she is playing softball.

Daddy stands firmly against Caroline's right side, his right hand clasping her shoulder. Caroline thinks about her last turn in the softball game at school. She hit that ball so high and far that she made it all the way to third base before Marcel was able to hurl the ball back in return. All weekend Caroline has been thinking about that hit, because it was not so much how hard she swung, but how soft the ball felt on impact. Caroline replays that cushy feeling in her mind.

28

<u>Persuasive Essay</u>
Caroline Carter
5th Grade

Children of divorced parents are not usually given choice of were they go. I think kids who are 13 years old should get a choice. Three reasons why I think they should are: the divorce wasn't their fault, they're responsidle, and independent.

Thirteen-year-olds are independent, and are young adults. They are old enough to know were they want to go because they are intelligent and knowledgeable. They're too old for their parents to make their decions. Also they have a right to too be given a choice on were they want to go.

Children of divorced parents should get a choice of were they want to go because the divorce was not their fault and the parents choose it. Also the kid wasn't the problem and He/She didn't want it. They should abe pick were they want to go because they didn't chooce the divorce.

Kids who are about 13 years old and of divorced parents are usually responsible enough and are young abults. The have responsibilities from caring for a sibling, cleaning the house, does all school work on time and keep grabes up.

Teenagers should choose were they want to go because they're young abults, the divorce wasn't there fault, and they are responsible.

29

Is Candyish Cereal Nutritious?
Caroline Carter
5th Grade

<u>Hypothesis</u>: I think the candyish cereal would be more nutritious because I would have more bowls and that would mean I would have more milk than one bowl of Cherrios or Bran Flakes.

<u>Candyish Cereal:</u> Trix, Lucky Charms, Fruity Pebbles

I think there will be a low Iron in Trix. I just know it from reading the boxes of healthy cereals.

<u>Background information</u>: Nutrition in candied and non-candied cereal. Candied cereal has 7 to 8 grams more sugar then a non-candied cereal. The non-candied has more vitamins and minerals then all of the candied cereals. On March 15, 6:15 a.m., I compared 2 bowls of Trix to 1 bowl of Bran Flakes. What's the most nutritious? Trix is more nutritious. On March 16, 8:00 a.m., I compared 1 bowl of Lucky Charms to 1 bowl of Bran Flakes. What's the most nutritious? Bran Flakes are more nutritious because there is one more mineral. On March 16, 6 p.m., I compared 1 bowl of Fruity Pebbles to 1 bowl of Bran Flakes. What's the most nutritious? Bran Flakes are.

<u>Procedure</u>: I ate the cereal and wile I was doing that I looked to see how much nutrition there was in the

cereal. Next I compared to see how much nutrition was in Bran Flakes and Trix, Lucky Charms and Bran Flakes, and Fruity Pebbles and Bran Flakes. I also wrote down how I felt after eating the cereal and if I had alot of energy.

March 15	6:15 a.m.	2 Bowls of Trix
March 16	8:00 a.m.	1 Bowl of Lucky Charms
March 16	6:00 p.m.	1 Bowl of Fruity Pebbles

Conclusion: On the first day, the candyish cereal was more nutritious because I had two bowls. I felt great and jumpy. I had a lot of energy to do my work at school. There was not a lot of Iron in the Trix. On the morning of the second day, the Bran Flakes were more nutritious because phosphorous, magnesium and copper were not in Lucky Charms. I felt exactly the same as on the first day except I wasn't jumpy. I wasn't jumpy because I had two bowls of Trix on the first day and one on the second. On the evening of the second day, I had Fruity Pebbles. I felt great, except a little tired. Fruity Pebbles wasn't as nutritious as the other two cereals.

30

Over the copper pans hanging on the kitchen wall, Mommy attaches a plastic Happy Graduation banner with snowing confetti. The banner marks the spot under which Caroline's wooden homework table has remained since kindergarten. Long outgrown as a place for productivity, it is now a way station for class projects deposited the night before school. Mommy uses one of the wood child chairs for her purse. Caroline uses the other for her backpack. Today the small table has Caroline's school books to return and a baseball.

Caroline wears her first off-the-shoulder dress. Its wide white bib marks a thick swatch around her shoulders and chest. Two shoulder straps provide anchor. Extra material cossets around Caroline's midriff. The skirt falls to mid-calf. Caroline wears new flats with no socks. Standing next to her tiny homework table with the chairs that just reach her knees, Caroline happily obliges Mommy with a smile. Caroline has her graduation present, a baseball glove, on and raised to her chest with her other hand tucked in the ready. On the wallpaper behind Caroline, white daisies explode in innumerable, clustered bouquets from an aqua background.

* * *

Reading someone else's diary offers the thrill of voyeurism, tinged with the suspicion that what we read may not be the sworn truth. What about the temptation to rewrite history to suit our egos, our reputations or our pocketbooks? Some diarists, in recognition of the momentousness of their times or their status or both, write for posterity. Some for vindication. Some, engaged in commercial or subsidized ventures, want to present the best news to investors.

The diary is far from "an artless transcription of reality," say Dan Doll and Jessica Munns in Recording and Reordering. Rather, "the diary writer always serves as an editor as well as a composer: a diary can never offer absolutely unmediated experience. There is always a principle of selection."[21] Which isn't to say that every diary is a pack of lies, though some may well be. Along those lines, public officials and their memoirs must be read with a grain of salt. William Safire puts it bluntly. In his 1994 *New York Times* essay "On Keeping Diaries," he declares, "Though always self-serving and often too sloppy to be evidence, diaries of public officials help us estimate 'how it really was.'"[22] We must read with the understanding that these entries are "a first-draft impression" and "always self-serving."[23]

As with our officials, so with ourselves. What we are reading is Emilie Davis' *Civil War*, Anne Frank's Nazi occupation, and Samuel Pepys' *Great Fire*, filtered through their biases, beliefs, hopes and hatreds.

---

[21] Doll, Dan and Jessica Munns. "Introduction." *Recording and Reordering: Essays on the Seventeenth- and Eighteen-Century Diary and Journal*, edited by Dan Doll and Jessica Munns, Bucknell University Press, 2006, p. 10.

[22] Safire, William. "Essay; On Keeping Diaries." *New York Times,* Section A, 18 Aug., 1994, p. 23, www.nytimes.com/1994/08/18/opinion/essay-on-keeping-diaries.html.

[23] Ibid.

31

At Lily's lake cabin. Went swimming even though was really sort of cold. Had a picnic. Sorry if this is a mess, but writting in dark!

Went on a picnic. Rowed out to an island to eat. Just me and Lily went. Went swimming 4 times today. My sunburn kills.

Tempature was in 80's. Went in swimming a lot. Boy, it really is hot here. But I'd rather be here than at home.

Lily had cousins visit. We played with them. Really hot. Sweaty all day. Lily's Dad set off firecrackers.

We walked to the end of the road to the hard top. When we were coming home some boy ran after us and threw rocks.

I found a <u>red</u> hair in me! Boo! Hoo! Last day at the lake. Boo! Hoo! Have a club S.A.G. Secret Accociation Goners.

32

First day of sixth grade. Mr. Rebenka is nice. Don't really like the organization of the school. My old school was better.

Tests of math add, sub. No other teachers. Everybody, girls, have shoulderbags. Fire drill too. New kid, Barbara bugs me.

Had another Math Test, had a lot of them. Played with everyone in the KittyCat Club. Talked about slumber partys. Won't bring Fluffy.

Saw a movie on how to behave on busses. Real funny. My turn in school to do a salute & song, pick a song. Did a quotation too. Played with Lily.

Went to church at 9:30 instead of 11:00. I think better cause I get out then at 11:30 and so does Rita.

Had gym and music. In music sang jazzy song. Snapped fingers to song. Had kick ball game. Lost 2-3. We caught a lot of fly balls. Dad gone on trip.

Really don't like Mr. Rabenka, he yells at you when you accidently do something. Found a dead pigion with a band around it's leg.

33

Decided to write now that I am in 7th grade because boys are getting interesting in my life. One thing, no one in school even looks my way (boys)! What's wrong? I just hope when I'm about 16-17, like in books, I'll have a boy.

Mom called me a bubble, said "like Mom bubble like daughter bubble." I love Mom, she's so understanding and so funny. Sorry this is messy but writing in the dark. I still have hope. Marcel said hi to me and Dale Madden lit my bunson burner for me . . .

Dads not like Mom at all, no understanding! I'm planning to be a sitter, so I got a book out of the library called "The Baby Sitters Guide." I'm really learning a lot. No great things happened about boys.

No experiences with boys, cuz had to go to Nanas. Boy! I had fun telling (Listening) to dirty jokes with Harry and Andy.

No school. Study Day. It rained all today, last nite, tonite too! No encounters with boys. I wish something would happen like kids write in their diaries, "Marcel is dreamy, and he likes me!" Too bad it isn't true!

I curled my hair last night and today didn't want to go to school cuz of it!

I sort of don't like Dad. I was saying to Mom, "He takes away T.V. and he came in (after I goed away) and asked what I was talking 'bout. Poor Dad. I hope when I am 16 yrs I'll have a boyfriend.

Does Rita hate me? She isn't like she used to be, we really aren't friends. She is still to me the best friend I ever had! Hope she doesn't hate me! She just ignores me. I can't understand it. Janet is going to ask for me (inconspicuously).

I've planned to buy another ring (friendship) for Rita cuz she lost her other one. Maybe that's why she's not playing with me; she doesn't have a ring! No encounters with any boys 'cept Harry and Andy. Went over to Nana's.

I got Rita another Friendship ring, and I hope she likes it cuz it cost $4.88. She ignored me today too! It really is sort of depressing. I said "Hi Rita" and she said "Hi" and walked off! Well I never!

I bought a ticket for the dance. I sure do hope I do better than the last two dances. 1st dance—no one. 2nd—2 guys. Janet's pretty popular! I wish I were more likeable. What's wrong? Am I growing up too fast for their liking?

Dance! UGG, was terrible! No one danced with me. Am I too tall, most of the kids asked were short. Oh it's so depressing, no boy likes me! Marcel was their. If only he'd picked me! I've given up on Rita. I can live without her Humph!

It's really getting like spring! The air is cool and no steam comes from your mouth. I guess Rita refuses to like me, maybe I am terrible, but some guys like me so I mustn't be that bad!

Big 55-point quiz! Got to get all right! I got some furniture from Nana's house: burrow and desk. The burrow is really big and roomier.

34

A new ice cream store, Friendlies, opened today! Better than the one downtown. All the <u>kids</u> go there and it's not all filled with smoking teenagers! We have to go to Nana's tomorrow. All we do is sit around and suffer with headaches.

We had a family walk. I didn't want to go but when we got to the pond and walked around it, it turned out o.k. Went to Friendlies. It's neet there, Grownups go there too.

I stayed up to quarter past 9 ½ hour nine (9:45) copying over report. I started at 7:00 and whent to that time. Martin L. King (Dr.) is dead.

Isn't it terrible M.L. King Dr. is dead. Cryed in bed last nite. I was so sad. Shot in the head! Riots everywhere Wash D.C. lootings and fires! Rita not mad at me anymore! We have made up! I think she is so neet now! SIGH! I'm really happy. Then I think about Dr. M. L. K. and sad.

Didn't go to Nana's. Supposed to play with Rita, but she went shopping and I played with Janet. I feel sort of guilty cuz played with Janet when Rita was going to call me. I hope she didn't!

Really warm out. I keep thinking about Dr. M.L. K. and sort of cry, he was preaching for non-violence and was shot. <u>Contrast</u>.

Got 3rd term marks. Math—B Engl—B Science—B Music—B. No marks in French this term. Secretly took Home Ec dress home and now I have to bring it back to work on it for tomorrow. Smartie!

I got an A in Soc Studies! C to an A. Dr. Martin Luther King's funeral, really sad. And I cried alittle watching it (at home!). Went over Janet's to work on Fruit Fly report.

Went over Janet's today, too. Worked on Fruit fly reports. Moms really neet. Janet think too, cuz she's going to type out the whole report! I got a shot at school for chicken pox.

I can't wait to be in the fashion show at school. All I have left is the sleeves and hem. I'll go and do that tomorrow. Mom did my whole neck! She's a neet, cool, understanding guy.

I can't be in the fashion show! Mrs Herbert wouldn't let me take my dress home! (I am really sad). She said I could sew to show Mom and Dad, the nerve of her. Tried Dippidy Doo on my hair so won't be bushy. Hope works!

Got a haircut. Short! Janet says looks funny. She should keep her mouth shut, might hurt guys feelings (not me).

35

Posing on Nana's deck, Caroline's eyes are clear, her smile easy. She has taken off her glasses for this second photo. Caroline's left hand rests across her faded blue jean shorts, protecting what is inside that pocket. Mom is beside her. Dad, taller, is behind, one hand on his wife's shoulder, the other on the crook of Caroline's neck. Dad is caught in a moment of tentativeness, not quite smiling.

* * *

Caroline has accompanied me in my diary entries. She has held my hand and provided a measure of safety. She's my side-by-side friend. Caroline's company has allowed me to sit with myself, alongside predatory undercurrents that have been with me since I was very young and that visit me still.

It will be seven years before the next photo album snapshot.

Seven years that will include hair conditioning, summer sunburns, softball, Clearasil, Spring musicals and Winter Messiah sings, Senior Lifeguard lessons culminating in a terrifying underwater wrestle with Caroline's male swim coach as Caroline tests on a rescue hold and instead has to pull on the coach's armpit hair to release herself, a surprise sweet sixteen birthday party, a remarkable dream of a horse with a cartoon-wide mouth and teeth that leaves Caroline throbbing, slumber parties instead of proms, and waitressing at the town Greek restaurant, where Caroline gets a crush on one of the owners, who goes after an even younger waitress instead.

I, too, will enter puberty. What identities will I shed, like my monthly menses, cast off like the cells from my root cap as I grow deeper into the soil? The white snake has been dormant, but becomes more active now in its white, freshly sloughed skin.

PART III:
WHITE SNAKE SLOUGHING

One might assume United States presidents would keep a diary. But that's not always the case, therefore we have the President's Diarist, a National Archives and Records Administration employee who, according to The White House Historical Association and several presidential digital libraries, assembles documents found in Secret Service logs, the president's schedule, the president's daily briefing of intelligence reports, daily staff notes and incoming and outgoing telephone calls (the president's private line not included) to create a record of what the president does, where the president goes, whom the president sees, and sometimes, what was talked about. This assemblage, called The President's Daily Diary, is not to be confused with a president's personal diary, and begs the meaning of ghost-writing.

While we may adore the writings of Virginia Woolf and the literary elite of her time, Woolf herself adored the relationship she had with her entries in her diary, writes H. Porter Abbott in *Inscribing the Daily: Critical Essays on Women's Diaries*.[24] In it, she used a loose,

---

[24] Abbott, H. Porter. "Old Virginia and the Night Writer: The Origins of Woolf's Narrative Meander." *Inscribing the Daily: Critical Essays on Women's Diaries*, edited by Suzanne L. Bunkers

stream-of-consciousness style, which facilitated her formulation of her modernist fiction. Lynn Z. Bloom, in her essay "I Write for Myself and Strangers," quotes Woolf reveling in the oscillating nature of her ideal diary form, a "loose knit, & yet not slovenly, elastic so it will embrace any thing solemn, slight or beautiful that comes into my mind. I should like it to resemble some deep old desk, or capacious hold-all, in which one flings a mass of odds & ends without looking them through."[25]

In a diary, we not only record who we are; we can also define who we are. "Anaïs Nin ... in many ways is her 150-volume diary," Lynn Z. Bloom asserts."[26] Nin wrote in her diary for self-invention, Bloom argues, sometimes changing details of social occasions to construct a portrait that blurred fact and fiction and that, in fact, jumpstarted her novels, short stories and erotica.

---

and Cynthia A. Huff, University of Massachusetts Press, 1996, pp. 236-251.

[25] Bloom, Lynn Z. "'I Write for Myself and Strangers': Private Diaries as Public Documents." *Inscribing the Daily: Critical Essays on Women's Diaries*, edited by Suzanne L. Bunkers and Cynthia Huff, University of Massachusetts Press, 1996, p 29.

[26] Ibid., p. 23.

36

Diary, I have found something to write about now that I am in 8th grade. I went to Jr. Sociables and I danced all the days. I was with a boy all the time! Best of all, I danced a slow one (bearhug). Just before the guy came over, I was wishing someone would do it to ME! Well, someone did, his name is Teddy and that's all I know. He's in my homeroom but that's all. Boys I like: Dale Madden, Andy Willson, Scott Long (I know he likes me too cuz at a party at Lori's, he danced with me the whole time) and Teddy. Marcel was there too. Oh, I really think he's kool, but we are both are too shy to ask each other (he probably doesn't like me). I think he's scared it might get around the neighborhood. UGG! I'm going to socialize more with Lori cuz she knows all the boys mentioned. Mom said I have to be careful because I have extra-long legs and I drag the boys behind in couple dancing. Geesh!

37

Dad made fun of me cuz didn't read French so good. Says after a year, didn't learn a thing, says I'm stupid! I hate him, too! Asked Mom bout Homework, and she yelled at me. She told me to take the garbage out. Got dressed and came down but Dad already took it out. She said I should be ashamed of myself! ICK! I hate MOM! She doesn't even know what I am talking about half the time she argueing with me! Wouldn't let me go out cuz thought too dark! Couldn't go out after supper on a Sat. nite! (Not school nite)

38

Ahhhh . . . a new diary for the new me. Sixteen and I really love being a girl, and I like feeling like a girl. I think right at this point in your life it is very important to establish to yourself the kind of woman you would like to be. Seems to me that the older you get, the more important it is to become stable in what you want out of life and what life wants from you. Mom said that by the age of 30 you have finally figured out who you are. Thinking on that line, I probably will end up being a totally different person from what I am now. That is funny to think about because I seem to have put a lot of thought and, God, a lot of effort it seems into stabilizing myself. But to think that I am just going to change, after all my hard work trying to be just one kind of person. I am satisfied with myself, funny how in a couple of years I will seem awful childish and naive. Truthfully I don't want to lose all the childishness yet, I don't want to grow up all the way. Right now I want to be able to relapse into silliness and giggles if I feel like it, because I know in a couple of years it will be out of the question. I will be too old. That is sad that you have to give up part of yourself when you mature, just for the sake of maturing. But I guess you can look at it and say that it would be impossible to live with all the tension and responsibility if you didn't change. I think it's still sad.

39

I use this diary to relieve any tensions I may have before I go to bed. That way I can fall asleep better, and quicker, and have nothing bothering me. So the things that are bothering me are not unique—they are the everyday problems of an almost 17-year-old high school girl. Gee, I would like to think of myself with a little individualism. If you don't feel special to yourself, it is really hard to live, because no one else will feel they can accept you if you don't. I really feel you have to find yourself, or you just won't be happy. I'm glad I have found myself for now. I know I will change again, do more growing up and maturing, but for now I am satisfied and happy with myself.

Expectations for tomorrow: Finish last (great!!) critical essay on *Jane Eyre*

Lunch with cousins
Lavez la cheveux!!

40

the snow is falling.
It is crawling
Down night's fingers.
Stop — It lingers
on it's way down,
To wipe the frown
off a sad face.
Then continues ~~in its race~~ in its race
To the cold ground.
Now ain't that profound

I had to make it rhyme.

41

What a beautiful blustery day. I love windy days because it makes my cheeks red and my hair blow and I feel very pretty. I have finally found out what I want to be, what kind of girl I want to be, but I am just not satisfied. Why? Because in order for me to be completely a girl, I must react with men. And I do not. I do not have any verbal contact with boys generally at all. No boys usually make a point of talking to me. If I continue I am sure I could become extremely upset, but I really am not going to be a martyr about this. As every girl, I want to love someone. I am a romantic, face it. I don't want to wait. But as it seems as though I must, I have to find something else to take up my time. God, it is really hard but you can't let it get you down, everyone else has had this problem, God, I'm not the only one.

42

I want to talk, but I don't want to bring up things that hurt me. Crying with Fluffy isn't helping, so I will tell you. We were singing in the auditorium and Marcel and his new girlfriend walked in and were really enjoying <u>themselves</u>. I was really hurt because I have always liked Marcel but he never liked me. I have to admit that I still had hope. Now I don't. I learned today that he has gone to bed with some other girl. I don't know him hardly at all—he certainly isn't the kid I thought he was. He has really changed. The thing that hurt me was that I realized I would never be close to him. I guess in high school it seems like I am not going to be close to any boy—certainly not junior year!! I really have to work sometimes not to let it get me down. In sex-ed I learned that you are at your sexual peak in adolescence. So what do I do? Nothing. I just don't even have any special <u>friends</u> that are boys—let alone boyfriends. I get discouraged, like now. I try to say it doesn't matter—but it does! No matter how hard I try to justify to myself that I don't need one, I know I will never be totally convinced. Things just don't work out. It really is depressing to think I have to wait. And because I have nothing, I always dream I will, and hope I'll meet some neet kid at an exchange concert, dance, party, out of town friend's house, but nothing comes of it except a big letdown. It is so hard to bear sometimes. I am fine with girls. Just not with boys. How awful it is going to be to sit at home the night of the senior prom.

43

I finally vented my anger. Poor Mom. She tried to untangle my irrational and contradictory needs while I tried every put down in the book. I wanted relief from my depressing unhappiness. Mom became depressed because I seemed to be saying that I didn't think it right that I was unhappy—that I expected happiness. I don't like growing up when it means compromising the ideals you have until now lived by. I am very much afraid of losing myself in the compromise. Mom says that even if we strive, we won't always succeed, but we should still strive, hoping for the time when it will be right and success will come. I am afraid of ideals now. I don't want to preach persistence because I am afraid of continued failure. Mom says you must strive for the ideal, but accept that which most closely resembles it, because you will never reach the ideal. I am afraid.

44

I'm tight
I try to smile
But my eyes darten
instead

My breath quickens
As my hand touches

What
what am I saying?
What is it
That is holding me so?

* * *

Diaries are a place to probe the darkness. We use
them to exorcise our demons, or at least shake hands
with them. A diarist, says Helen Garner, wants to "get a

read of something that's making you unhappy, try to analyze it and take the sting out of it." [27] Known for her frank and unsparing detail, Garner, the Australian novelist, short-story writer, screenwriter and journalist, says in her 2016 interview with *Literary Hub* that, for this reason, "people tend not to write down their happiest experiences."[28] Writing on the diary as literature, Steven Kagle concurs. "The life of a diary is often born of tension, a disequilibrium in the life of the author, which needs to be resolved or held in check."[29]

The humorist David Sedaris takes a different approach to personal feelings. He doesn't trust them. Introducing a volume of his diaries from 1977–2002, he eschews the self and its accompanying feelings for observational "theft."[30] Sedaris is interested in "events (fistfights, accidents, a shopper arriving with a full cart of groceries in the express lane)," gossip, overhead conversation, found photos, pages torn from a magazine, bits of trash picked up off the street, the plot

---

[27] Garner, Helen. "Helen Garner on Court Burning Diaries and the Violence of Love: John Freeman in Conversation with the Author of *Everywhere I Look*," interviewed by John Freeman, *Literary Hub*, 27 September, 2016. lithub.com/helen-garner-on-court-burning-diaries-and-the-violence-of-love/.

[28] Ibid.

[29] Kagle, Steven E. *American Diary Literature, 1620-1799.* Twayne Publishers, 1979, p. 17.

[30] Sedaris, David. *Theft by Finding: Diaries 1977-2002.* Little Brown and Company, 2017.

of a soap opera. "[Feelings] weren't that interesting (even to me) but mainly because they were likely to change. Other people's feelings, though, that was a different story. Got a bone to pick with your stepmother or the manager of the place where you worked until yesterday? Please, let's talk!"[31]

---

[31] Ibid, p. 3.

45

Hello my confiding friend!! A nice thing happened today. Dad came into my room and suddenly he was telling me about all these things that happened to him during Air Force training. He was curled up on my bed and I was listening at my desk, where I had been working. It was a nice time because we were talking like friends, he had no misgivings about talking to me. I felt really good that Dad could feel free enough to sit and just talk. I think he enjoyed it, too. I know how Mom can love him. Sometimes he is so tight that he gets really irritable. He tries to hold a lot of tension inside and doesn't talk about it. So eventually it comes out in grumpiness. I could never understand that he is really an understanding person who is willing to talk things out and listen. I know if I ever got into trouble, he is so level-headed and understanding that I could come to him for help.

46

Sat   Here are 3 poems I wrote. They don't express what I feel, my
aim wasn't that. It was to write more maturely using symbols + images. I
feel really unsure.

Through pools of water I walk
My past fading away in the ripples of time.
The farther I walk,
The closer I get to the dry sand
Where empty shells preside.
I cannot walk fast,
The water is too deep
But it does not matter.
I have time enough
To make it to the other side
Before the sun goes down
And leaves me with the fleeting ripples
And the dry sand

The little green car
That took me to the supermarket
The movies
The winter clearance sale
The free painting lessons
And the French resterant
Has been replaced by
A long black one.

They listened
As the words came flooding out
And ran over my lap
On to the floor.
They stared
As my voice
Crept higher and higher up my throat
And grasped on to me
And cut me off
So I could speak no more
And then they looked away.

Saturday

Sunday

47

Why is it just because I got my license Dad is getting really annoyed whenever I want to drive? I wanted to go to the library—God, Dad has a way about him. He says something like—just because I don't walk to the library is not a good enough reason for you not to. Just cause you have your license you think you can take the car anywhere. So I get mad and decide not to go at all. Then he goes and gives me the big story: "If you're really pressed for time..." and makes me feel like an ass that I even thought about using the sacred object. True, all I wanted to do was drive, but how am I supposed to learn and practice. Some days I want to talk about sex. Ever since that first meeting of the sex-ed course, I have become slowly but surely aware. I have noticed feelings in myself, and I have also noticed when Mom and Dad have sex. Is it cuz I am noticing or cuz they are doing it more or cuz I am up later? But I don't see how anyone could have missed it tonight—it was so loud. At first I thought something was wrong but then I realized what was going on—the sexy little buggers. Tomorrow will be my day to be feminine—if I ever get to bed! I washed my hair in the

shower and shaved my legs and its now 11:00.
Love = Jane.

48

Oh, have faith in me yet, dear diary, I have not given up, neither should you.

Lily just told me something so far out that I was struck really emotion-less. She said she was in love with one of her teachers, and truthfully the feeling was likewise. More, he felt stronger feelings for her than for his wife of 9 years! Oh, Lily I don't think you can handle this. She is thinking of marriage—this is serious, God, it is. She says they are spiritually—What if she has sex with him? How old is this guy? He's in his 30's. Oh God, Lily. I don't know what to say. She has talked with "Dennis" about the whole thing. But it's wrong. I have the feeling—I know it's going to be bad. He probably has said more to Lily than his wife. I don't think Mr. Dunn is being too smart. I feel so worried. I can't talk to anyone, Lily trusts me to keep still, not only for her, but for "Dennis." Is Lily responsible enough to handle such a situation? Does Mrs. Dunn know anything about this?

I didn't want to say anything to Lily about my reservations because I don't know what to do.

Please, I'm all mixed up. I have a feeling this is wrong somehow, but it is not my place to interfere. I don't know enough. I don't have the experience. God, I don't even know the love between a man and a woman. Lily says with Mr. Dunn she feels safe. That is part of love. I wish I knew love like others do. The love I hold onto selfishly through friends is not enough. God, I want more!!! Oh please, I am so tired of waiting for somebody to come. I want, need must have love soon. I am finding it hard to live without it. Like this, I feel empty sometimes. I am alone. How long am I to wait for this "natural" thing to occur. Oh, I am lost without love. Lost.

49

I have been near tears all day. Life seems so relentless. Here it is the middle of spring vacation and already I am tormented with the tensions of homework. Why, God, does this have to bother me so much. I am really on edge!

Well, I feel better now that Mom and Dad are home and things are going OK. and the day has ended with hope for tomorrow. As Lily would say: Whee! I am so glad to have Lily as a friend! I get really happy to think we have gotten so close. Whee!

50

Lil here. I just couldn't resist writing something to ya, since tonight your mother will be with us in the car and we won't be able to talk . . . SO this is why you just caught me writing in here!! (whoops!) anyways . . .

Wow wow wow wow wow you remember I was talking to you about Denny? Wow I can't even describe what this truthful thing is between us wow!! Just be satisfied to know that I feel so beautiful—and, when you have a—I mean, when your life is actually part of someone else's mind, it's so BEAUTIFUL! It can't be described! Just take my word for it: I'm feeling so fantastic. I don't want you to worry about me. <u>Really</u>. I've never been more together than now. I'd rather you be happy for me, and with me. Ok? Really—you don't have cause to worry—I'll talk to you more later, cuz I'm using up your diary.

51

Dear Lily, I hope to God that you are together. Truly, I want to be happy for you so much but your situation is so screwed up that it can't work out. Oh, Lily. I hope you come out of this all right. I don't know. I would think Mr. Dunn would have enough control not to fall in love (I still find it really hard to believe that it is love—yet I believe Lily) once he is married. I have to remember now what Mom said. She felt that love isn't this "fate" thing where you were destined to love just one man. You can fall in love with many. Once you are married, you just have to not let yourself get into situations where love could flourish.

I really feel Mr. Dunn is in the wrong, by playing upon the naiveté of Lily. I know that at my stage now, I would feel the same way as Lily. Yet Mr. Dunn really must be crazy to lead Lily on for his pleasure (and Lily's too) when he knows it just won't work out. I don't know what to do, because Lily realized that the situation is really screwy, but she is blinded by her happiness. I am just holding my breath and waiting.

52

Jane Eyre. I really love that story so much. There is so much personality to each of the characters. I don't want to hold too much importance on the book, but I really admire how Jane was able to stand up as an equal to Mr. Rochester and hold to her values, even if that meant leaving the only love she knew. I don't think I could of done that. I would be swept away by my emotions. I'm afraid. Sometimes I get scared about a relationship. God, I want one, yes, but I'm afraid that since I have never had one, I won't be able to keep my own identity with a boy. What I mean is that I will do whatever the boy wants because I will want him to like me so much that I will be afraid to disagree and I will lose my identity. That would not be cool.

* * *

Self-inscription can come to a diarist at any time. It can be a tool of reckoning, a stock-taking of our lives as they have unfolded. At the age of ninety, the Welsh historian and essayist Jan Morris began keeping a diary for the first time, feeling inspired to make entries sometimes twice a day to reflect on literature, the arts, current affairs, and history.[32] The American poet, novelist and memoirist May Sarton, in her diary "At Seventy," calls this point of reference "growing into age."[33] Virginia Woolf kept a diary as a young girl, being pegged by her family as the "unofficial historian" for her highly personal entries. Ernest Hemingway kept a diary as a young boy at Oliver Wendell Holmes Elementary School, successfully anticipating that "I intend to travel and write."[34] Journalist Simon Akam, in a First Person piece for Paris Review in 2013, recalls he started as a diarist when he was six, calling these early entries of children the "record-of-your-holiday-please" school assignment.[35]

---

[32] Morris, Jan. *In My Mind's Eye: A Thought Diary.* Faber & Faber, 2018.

[33] Sarton, May. *At Seventy: A Journal.* Norton, 1984.

[34] "Famous Diary Entries: 9-Year-Old Hemingway Intends to 'Travel & Write.'" *Endpaper,* 9 April, 2013, blog.paperblanks.com/2013/04/famous-diary-entries-hemingway/.

[35] Akam, Simon. "The Diary Diaries." *The Paris Review,* 10 October, 2013, www.theparisreview.org/blog/2013/10/10/the-diary-diaries/.

53

The violets are up in our yard! I would like to
press one here. Almost graduation!!

I have time to write
Time to think
Time to fight
For the link
To my identity
An entity
Which is very hard to see.

54

I have a stomach
That grows bigger when I eat.
     I can't stop the treats.
Tomorrow I begin another try
To get my pot back down to size
But it probably won't succeed,
'Cause none of the tries have ever taken seed
But I'm going to it with that same gung-ho
Hoping my stomach won't show!!

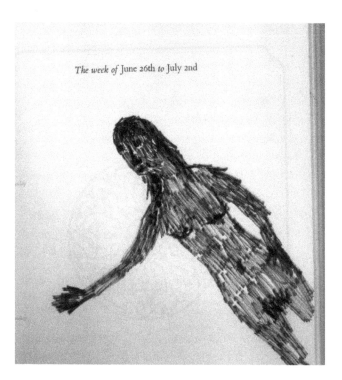

The week of June 26th to July 2nd

55

On Your Twentieth Birthday

Did I see it go by
All of it clear with unclouded
       eye
Through candles beneath the
       soft willow tree
By the shimmer and glare of
       the Atlantic sea?

Eyes bright in footlights,
Voice strong in song,
Arms stretching to heights,
Legs extending to long.

Did I see it all clearly?
What passed me by?
Were they candid shots merely
That caught my eye?

Body's shaping toward grace,
The changing face,
The laughter, the love,
What was beneath what I
       saw from above?

                    Mom

56

Last night I dreamt that I was back in high school. After 2 years of college I had to go back to finish my senior year and graduate. Funny that I can only find confidence from the past. I expressed the fear to Mom that I might become another Alma Thompson, a woman never married who is unhappy that way. Mom seemed to consider my fear as if it were a possibility.

57

* * *

The form a diary takes can be as episodic and routine as its daily enumeration or as open-ended and varied as the author's imagination. Daybooks are formatted into page-a-day preprints. Other diaries are written on slips of paper as if the ideas themselves have inconspicuously inserted themselves into the author's consciousness. The chosen form of a diary indicates something about the diarist. Sedaris uses 8 x 9 ½-inch plastic- or wire-bound volumes that lend themselves to his assemblage of artwork and collected mementos. Thoreau transposed his initial slips of paper to a hard-to-decipher handwritten diary, adding tabulated records, political outrage, and comments on his process, which in winter required the thawing of his ink.[36] Zickefoose, the ornithologist painter of hatchlings, swears by 20 x 30-inch sheets of 140-pound Fabriano or Winsor and Newton hot-press watercolor paper. "There's something about the smooth, quiet surface of hot-press paper that helps me relax and keeps me from noodling too much detail into the paintings."[37] With far less to work with, Nelson Mandela wrote his account of life in prison on a desk calendar. Nixon recorded his diary each evening on Dictabelt tapes. This "simultaneously elastic and tight" feature of diaries, their content "wide-ranging yet patterned," make them adaptable and flexible, note Suzanne L. Bunkers and Cynthia A. Huff in their introduction *to Inscribing the Daily: Critical Essays on Women's Diaries.*[38]

---

[36] Walls, Laura Dassow. *Henry David Thoreau: A Life,* University of Chicago Press, 2017.

[37] Zickefoose, Julie. *Baby Birds: An Artist Looks into the Nest.* Houghton Mifflin Harcourt, 2016, p. xix.

[38] Bunkers, Suzanne L. and Cynthia A Huff. "Issues in Studying Women's Diaries: A Theoretical and Critical Introduction." *Inscribing the Daily: Critical Essays on Women's Diaries,* edited by Suzanne L. Bunkers and Cynthia A Huff, University of Massachusetts Press, 1996, p. 1.

58

I receive a letter from home. Inside is a clipping, cut out and taped to a ripped-in-half sheet of lined paper.

From last Sunday's N.Y. Times Magazine. Parallels my thinking exactly. Love. Mom

If one of my daughters did tell me that she had begun an affair, I hope I'd be able to do this, was responding to clues from her own body, not to pressure from her fellow or her friends. I hope I'd be able to tell her the six ways to delay the arrival of my grandchild and I'd hope and expect that she already knew them. I think then I would tell her to count on the usual mixture of joy and pain that always comes with love. I hope she'd be brave enough, daring enough, to experience all the feelings of anxiety, mixed with pleasure, obsession and jealousy, tenderness and anger that must accompany any relationship of meaning. Everyone must spend some time being a slave of love. But, please, I would ask her, don't forget your work, your mind, your other activities. Don't drown in this relationship. I would hope that, for her, the end of the affair would not be too destructive or too filled with regret and hurt, and I'd want her to remember that *forever* is mostly for fairy tales. I would tell her that sexual excitements and satisfaction grow with experience and that she should not be disappointed if the beginnings don't meet her expectations—that she should be patient with herself and her friend and her physical pleasures will increase. And then I think I might go into my own room, close my door, and weep for the child whose genitals I had once wiped and covered with powder.

Drugs, alcohol or religious and political extremes can mushroom into nightmares that make sexual experimentation seem as harmless as stamp-collecting or other hobbies of the tranquil past. The other day, one of my daughters pointed a broom at me, cocked her head in the attitude of Patty Hearst and said, "Die, capitalist pig!" Ha, I laughed, or meant to laugh. Who, after all, knows where this innocent with her belief in justice for everyone may end? How can I choose her friends, hope she isn't insane enough to turn to violence, hope that she is insane enough to be comfortable with some of the insanities of the adult world, hope that the extremes of political cruelty on the left and the right don't drive her to cruelties of her own? My mother might have feared diseases contracted from toilet seats; I am afraid of the cultural air. I'm afraid of gurus and freaks of meditation, astrology and health foods. I can stay up all night with images of disasters that have already happened to the children of friends, neighbors to the left and neighbors to the right.

I find this newspaper clipping, so meticulously taped to the half sheet of lined paper, truncated. Who wrote this? Is the author left in a swirl of imaginative doom or was there more to the piece than what Mom sent? I tuck the clipping into my diary, where it yellows.

59

1/1
Woke up in clothes
Had doughnut & O.J.
Drove home
Ate B. fast so I could....
Give blood
Almost (!!) fainted

60

Dear Jane,

Well that does it . . . now they tell me coffee causes cancer of the pancreas. A person just can't be oral compulsive these days.

I'll tell you why you left Matt—'cause you cannot figure skate and when the intoxication of the chase is over he'll still want you to do that on top of being humorous, assertive, informed, exciting, and most of all adoring. In addition to that mentality which plagues a certain generation of men, there are also some problems (or were) that are "peculiar" to the coordination of you and Matt. It seemed to have something to do with both of you finding something lacking in each other that you didn't want to continue to go without. And with you it seemed to boil down to Matt always wanting you to perform for him and not being able to really share all your career goals and excitement. One thing that really sticks in my mind is that you did not want to actualize yourself through Matt.

I don't see how the hell you are managing to keep seeing him and not fall off the edge one way or another. In some ways I wish you felt as strong as you were when we last saw each other—getting on with your own life. On the other hand I like Matt and sometimes wonder if the problem isn't just the times and not the particular man.

Things here are difficult to describe. I'm pretty lonely on the personal friendship "lay your guts on the table" level but I do spend a lot of time with groups of women, for one reason and another, and get a lot of satisfaction out of finding so much frequent understanding between people who are not really close friends.

I hope school is going well for you and that the house is turning out to be a good family.

Much Love,

Rita

61

Jane, how nice to get your long thoughtful letter. It is, I must admit, a bit difficult for me to completely comprehend your meaning. You seem to be saying that you want to make a contribution in your field, do something unusually meaningful and something on a large scale, something that has influence. I think that's wonderful and can only shout, "Go for it!" I guess you know that involves being watchful for opportunities, being in tune with your own energy, and taking risks. It also means the possibility of failing and having to pick up and go for it again. So I know you know all this and I commend your courage. But I can't help wondering at the same time, why, while you are achieving in many less spectacular ways, you cannot feel encouraged by those times, too? Maybe you do. Maybe you do know that it is spectacularly creative to be a good friend and spectacularly intelligent to create time for isolation. So you need not be so hard on yourself lacking the large, noticeable accomplishments.

And, then again, what is all this talk about postponing personal commitments in order to fulfill these other goals? Is it really true that they cannot take place simultaneously? I really don't know. I'm asking. Is it true that those old human goals, like having someone to share it all with, can't be reached until we've made it on our own? Is it what your generation thinks? Do you really compartmentalize your lives so that personal fulfillment is something that must be done alone? Are you afraid of owing a debt if there are others around? That's what I really have trouble understanding. Why, at an age when energy is high, do you think that such a choice is necessary—that it might even be easier (less encumbering?) to go it alone? Do young people not realize the mathematics of the strengths of two amounting to more than the sum of the parts? Your letter has set me thinking because it does indicate a very different outlook which has taken place, and I am pondering the cause and also trying to comprehend it.

I think it is nice to have someone to depend on—and it's nice to know someone depends on me. It, frankly, has helped me do some of the things I've done. In many ways, it can be called a selfish thing. It is an odd idea to me that so many young people are rejecting such a simple need.

I love you, too.

Mom

62

Went to counseling today. Was talking about Oliver—something about him was bothering me. The counselor was asking me to say more, and I got to talking about his dense, dark beard, and how it reminded me of pubes and I guess I flooded out cuz all of a sudden, from far away I hear the counselor yelling: "Oh my God! Oh my God!" and I am just coming back and going "Wha?" while she is yelling: "Oh my God, what did he do to you?!" and I look at her blankly, and whatever I was in touch with is gone and I am looking at her blankly and she starts apologizing over and over.

Thanks a lot, 10-Free-College-Counseling-Sessions Counselor!

* * *

Simon Akam, the journalist who began as a diarist in school, itemizes the forms his diaries take, still stored in his boyhood bedroom:

My oldest journal is a 1992–93 'mid-year' diary… After a four-year hiatus, a series of page-a-days. . . Next come exercise books, one sheathed in a tan leather cover inset with porcupine needles, and a tranche of Moleskines. The final shift in format . . . the books become larger; eight by eleven inches. They are bound in quarter leather and the covers are marbled. The first bears in gilt script Simon Akam with a rough transliteration of my name in Arabic. New York 2008 appears further down. In short, a slightly embarrassing trajectory of increasing literary pretension.[39]

Some diaries are literally too hot to handle. Marie Curie's lab diaries are still so radioactive, they are stored in a lead-lined box in France's Bibliothèque Nationale. Those wishing to peruse the Pierre and Marie Curie Collection must do so in protective clothing, and only after signing a waiver of liability.[40]

When diaries are published, originally handwritten entries often are transcribed. On the other hand, publication format may appear as a facsimile of the original, as in #OldManDiary on Twitter, replete with the free-association drawings and notes. Or a published diary may include an itemized scrapbook or collage of

---

[39] Akam, Simon. "The Diary Diaries." *The Paris Review,* 10 October, 2013, www.theparisreview.org/blog/2013/10/10/the-diary-diaries/.

[40] O'Carroll, Eonin. "Marie Curie: Why Her Papers are Still Radioactive." *The Christian Science Monitor.* 7 November, 2011, https://www.csmonitor.com/Technology/Horizons/2011/1107/Marie-Curie-Why-her-papers-are-still-radioactive.

collected memorabilia prepared in folio fashion as an art book. Lee Lozano, a New York So-Ho artist, kept a diary from 1968 to 1972 and documented in eleven volumes quirky asides from her neighborhood daily life, interactions with friends, as well as reflections on gender politics and art's role in society. She wrote in thin wire-spiraled, pocket-sized dime store notepads which have been reproduced to exact size, color and format, including the spiral binding.[41] "There can be something very inspiring about seeing a cheap pocket notebook filled with handwriting that is by turns semi-interesting and mundane," says a Lozano diary reader. "It makes you feel like anyone could make a book, or at least fill a notebook in such a way that it looks like something."[42]

---

[41] Lozano, Lee. *Private Book 1*. Karma, 2017; Lee Lozano. *Private Book 2*. Karma, 2017; Lee Lozano, *Private Book 3*. Karma, 2017; Lee Lozano, *Private Book 4*. Karma, 2018; Lee Lozano, *Private Book 5*. Karma, 2018.

[42] J. Zorker, email message to author, August, 28, 2018.

63

Dear Rita,

I am, as ever, single and (choose your least provocative word) alone, uninvolved, independent, on my own, struggling but sometimes uniquely happy. I did that solo improv piece to sound effects and music. Well-attended crowd. My idea was to bridge the gap between performer and audience, which was easier with the stage and audience on the same level. They found the piece comedic. Who knew?!

But my helplessness paper isn't moving. I thought I had it all wrapped up in a simple academic exercise after a brain-storm. HA! MAJOR PSYCHOLOGICAL BLOCK. ARGGGG!

I did go to a Halloween party, as The Milky Way. I took small, Styrofoam balls and coated them in glitter, then attached pipe cleaners to the glitter balls and then attached them randomly all over a long white slip so these glitter balls poked out oddly and at random. AND bounced when I moved. HA. The party was just OK.

So here I am. Twenty-seven years old. Home from grocery shopping. I wanted to be with someone, but no one I could think of fit exactly my mood. I tried a couple of people. No dice. Then you came to mind—yes, being with Rita. Because in all our grapplings over beer and popcorn, we both seemed to appreciate that amidst all the struggles, life goes on.

I love you — Jane

64

Train

(inside, angular)
(admissin)

Eyeballs

Contrast!
thru out
Δ in dynamic

flying

hair = angular
a chair

. techno .

lights

YEARNING?

Can I
use a
screen or
sheet?
I audience
sees my
shadow?

plexiglass
= body
Tensey

build-up to break
bar sounds

SLO MO Break thru

?

ody touching)
Hard

Black-
breathe / or finger clicking
as move ladder off stage
climbs up

Break thru

FUNNY? / SURPRISE Jump

- behind screen
Hi Energy ex: maniac, Rosanna
KTM: 456-1510

Larry Carlton

*Kim Sunny tate

Theme of linking - like play

connecting hands.
slapping thighs

maybe something funny about what is
in control, me or the object I'm
manipulating

65

Dear Parents,

I am writing to ask your permission to video-record your child as part of my research project, "Teacher Strategies in an Early Childhood Education Play Setting." I will use three cameras facing into the yard and two dropped microphones over the yard and out of the reach of children and adults. The cameras and microphones will be turned on as teachers prepare the yard each afternoon and will run every afternoon for two weeks.

Our circle times will talk about the camera equipment and what it will look like. My experience is that when the children are prepared ahead of time, they generally acknowledge the presence of research equipment but remain occupied with their activities.

My recordings will pick up the children's actions and words as they play, and the teachers' actions and words as they work with the children. All data will be kept locked and used solely for purposes of this research. Children's names will be changed in any resulting presentations, papers, and publications.

Whether you provide permission or not will not affect you or your child's standing in the school.

Jane Perry

66

I <u>don't</u> believe polls that say that the majority of Americans accept the war as the solution. I also think that people in this country are so frightened because they feel themselves and the world out of touch and therefore out of control. Being out of control is fearful.

I know what it is like to hear so much incongruity from the outside world that I begin to doubt myself. A dangerous condition, because doubting oneself is a form of suppression about what you know to be true—yourself. And suppression of oneself leads to an apathetic shut-down, depressed state.

Each one of us has unlimited creative power. To suppress that power means to die spiritually. No wonder many people in this country are out of touch. I think they are dying spiritually.

So for me, this military crisis is a turning point. I know I am not spiritually dead. I am feeling my power. So there is at least one person who is spiritually alive. I also know that I am talking with others every day who are alive.

Don't forget how easy it is to feel isolated. Talk with other people whenever you can. Feel that they are alive. This is important for you.

67

A snorting. Breathing and snuffling against her side of the tent. What is outside and what is inside separated by taut, strong, albeit thin nylon. With those others in her tent too dense to notice,[43] she is left to ponder companionship and privacy. Her privacy really is about safety, learned so long ago that she does not question nor reconsider that what she fantasizes about is anything to share, except when she confuses a fantasy with fact.

This happened, in fact, with these others, at the dining room table over a frolicking dinner during a college break for her. They: all laughing.

"That's just like the time we rented an RV and drove to Florida!" she had said, continuing the roil of mirth.

The others: stopping in mid-gasp.

"Ah, Jane," the father says. "We never went to Florida."

But she can see the RV tires nestled in the powdery white sand.

Of course this family of hers would have never piled into an RV, let alone driven the length of the East Coast. So why the perfect conviction of this as a family fact?

---

[43] "But those others in her tent are too idiotic to notice." Alice Munro, "Child's Play." *Family Furnishings: Selected Stories, 1995-2014*. Alfred A. Knopf, 2014, p. 480.

Maybe because those others in this tent were too dense to notice then, too.

68

Know/Want/Learn Chart
Jane's Circle Time Ideas

What We Know About Hyenas	What We Want to Find Out About Hyenas	What We Learned
There's pokey things all over them. I'm scared of hyenas. They can eat you up. They are in cages. Don't put your fingers in the cage. Hyenas bite. What are the cages made of? Plastic. No! Metal. If you want to see the babies, you could. They are in cages, too. By themselves. Hyenas eat meat. We are meat. Hyenas also eat corn. And bones. Hyenas have legs. They have stripes. Or spots. Where is the cage?	How are we getting to the hyenas tomorrow? Are we going to walk? How hyenas eat corn? Do they eat it like us? What do they eat? Why are the Mommies and Daddies not with their babies? How many cages are there? Do they eat plants? What color are the cages? Will we hear the hyenas?	Hyenas eat corn. All of it. They snort. They jump high — their legs are strong. They have a yucky smell. That's because they pee. They pee in their cage. Their cage IS metal and blackish brownish and very strong. They look different than Lion King. They go "Whoop! Whoop! Whoop!" We took a bus and went up a hill to their cages.

* * *

The musician, actress and provocateur Courtney Love uses her memorabilia of personal letters, childhood records, poetry, diary entries (including a smear of lipstick and a doodled self-portrait), other original writings, song lyrics, fanzines, show flyers, and Polaroids for her diary. Billed as an "assemblage in disarray" by Lisa Levy of Salon, "actually closer to a yearbook for a school with only one graduate,"[44] *Dirty Blonde: The Diaries of Courtney Love* became public in a published, glossy-paged art facsimile.[45] With the emergence of digital media, libraries make diaries of note available online as scanned documents, deciphering of handwriting left to the reader.

Blogging has let anyone and everyone go public with their self-inscriptions. Developmental neurotoxicology and cancer epidemiology researcher Brooke Magnanti published an anonymous 2003 diary blog, belledujour.[46] She described in quips of conversation, snippets of encounters, and an enumerated listing of daily tasks her life as a doctoral student with a side job at a London escort service.

---

[44] Levy, Lisa. "The People vs. Courtney Love." *Salon.* 6 November, 2006, 5:30 p.m., www.salon.com/2006/11/06/courtney_scrapbook/.

[45] Love, Courtney. *Dirty Blonde: The Diaries of Courtney Love.* Faber & Faber. 2007.

[46] Gallagher, Paul and Peter Walker. "Belle du Jour Blogger Unmasks Herself as 'Big-Mouthed Boyfriend' Looms." *The Guardian, 15* November, 2009, www.theguardian.com/technology/2009/nov/15/belle-de-jour-author-blogger-brooke-magnanti.

Twitter and Instagram feature diaries. Some are anonymous. Some are family: "My Aunt Bee's African travel journal is full of illustrations & observations. I feel honored to read it!" says travel author Tui Snider.[47] The poet Mira Gonzalez and Tao Lin the novelist, short story writer, and memoirist have together amassed nearly 40,000 diary-formatted tweets which are published into a leather-bound, illustrated book where on one side are Gonzalez's tweets and, flipped over, are Lin's.[48] There is even a video game in diary format, *Diaries of a Spaceport Janitor*, albeit fictional, that operates within the routine of trash disposal, with no reward or penalty for either occupying the mundanity of this daily job or breaking out of it by disengaging a cloying Annoying Skull curse.[49]

Want to not only inscribe your thoughts, but share your voice with the world? Podcasts are a natural medium for diarists who love to hear themselves talk. Like the written diary, these audio diaries run the gamut, from bare-bones enumeration to full-out

---

[47] @TuiSnider. "My Aunt Bee's African travel journal is full of illustrations & observations. I feel honored to read it! " *Twitter,* 14 Aug 2018, 11:53 a.m., https://twitter.com/TuiSnider/status/1029440820204593152.

[48] Gonzales, Maria and Tao Lin. *Selected Tweets*. Ann Arbor, Short Flight / Long Drive Books, 2015.

[49] Porreca, Ray. "Diaries of a Spaceport Janitor Finds Meaning in the Mundane." *Destructoid.com*, 10 June, 2016, 14:00:00, www.destructoid.com/diaries-of-a-spaceport-janitor-finds-meaning-in-the-mundane-389875.phtml.

storytelling. There are money diaries, anxiety diaries, readings from childhood diaries, food diaries like Refrigerator Diaries, which relates food to a person's everyday life by itemizing what's inside, Muni Diaries–your place to share transit stories from San Francisco, and countless more. National Public Radio's podcast Radio Diaries gives people recorders and works with them to document their present lives. Less produced but still compelling in audio presence is spoken journals, like Maureen Ezeude's podcast Diary of a Bad Bitch, which follows a similar reflective format as in the written diary. Libraries are responding to the audio allure. The Morgan Library and Museum offers The Diary: Three Centuries of Private Lives, a series of online podcast readings from featured diaries in its archive.

69

Three Dreams in AM.

1. In my dream I am at the top of a snowy mountain getting ready to ski down. I really want to do this (versus other times in real life when I have been scared at the top) and I am impressed when I start that I have any control at all. Most important, I can control my speed and direction. The trail is thin and well-marked just like a cross-country trail. Clean and white. I sometimes go off the beaten path but I am able to keep my balance and find the path again without falling. I have the clear feeling if I just keep alert rather than be succumbed by fearful feelings, I can stay up rather than fall. I make it to the bottom. I am so thrilled, like a milestone, that I wake up to consciously celebrate this dream.

2. I am at Lily's lake cabin and we are crossing a dirt path (her mom may have been with us) when I turn around and notice Lily face down in the road, hurt. I cradle her like the game we used to play at her lake. My body and Lily's become one. If I just keep my legs open by sitting cross-

legged, then Lily doesn't bleed from her wound.

3. I am walking up a busy city avenue I know. It is dark. There is some kind of fight. Police cruisers arrive and I am arrested with others. I am feeling matter of fact. I don't feel guilty like I usually do if for any reason I am part of something wrong. I am accepting. I am feeling out of my element though, and odd. I huddle in my cell. It is too small to stretch out in. I am grateful when I notice a shower, though the water would go all over the foreshortened bed. I rinse myself off. I am told that I am in the wrong cell and I am taken to another area. It is a many-tiered, white-foam-covered, plastic arrangement of spaces for women. I have to climb up and around many other women's places to get to my space. I feel I am in a place of wise women who will have much to teach me about how to survive. I am meant to be here. These women have a lot of information for me. I have a nagging hair-thin splinter that is on my thumb. I have been trying to get it out for the longest time. A group of women are close around me. One has tweezers and easily and quickly pulls it out. I feel incredible relief. I

am surprised that finally, here, with all these women, my splinter comes out.

70

What Do Friends Do At School?
Jane's Circle Time Ideas

You can make them something.
Play and be gentle.
Make them warm.
Give them a hug.
Be goofy. Give them kisses.
Do their game. Their favorite game.
If you have an idea and someone else has an idea, you can put them together.

71

Preparing for the birth
Affirmation and Goals

I am enjoying time by myself to reflect and remember that I have everything I need in my life.

I am taking very good care of myself. I am in excellent health and my body knows exactly what it needs to do.

I realize that I am a little intimidated when I feel the baby pushing out from my body. I am feeling hard bumps like heels. This is real! Yikes. Do I want this baby? What if it is too much for me? Then I remember the baby came to us after I meditated on being ready for "the next step." It would be helpful to reread my journal back in July.

I didn't write in July. Oh well, the process is certainly clear enough. <u>Asking</u> for what I want with the <u>belief</u> that I will get it, and <u>accepting</u> it when it comes.

So maybe this new baby represents a concrete example of how my life <u>delivers</u> on requests. I certainly am creating. Creating is in my body. What an affirmative reminder about how accessible creating is in my life.

72

73

I stand naked, except for socks and sneakers, eating popcorn. Last night, milk-sweetened baby vomit dripped warmly down my back as I sat in a dark room cultivating how it aroused me. I shudder, recollecting how a friend had inadvertently made the sound of a delicate, half cry and I had laughed explosively loud and long in response.

My expectations for adventure have become a function of crowded habits. Finding a beer in the refrigerator that has been on its side for so long it is corroded on its base, but still opens with a satisfying hiss. Watching how a bromeliad without water for long periods will sprout appendages and feeling reassured that even in potential distress it grows. Leaving messages on my home machine from work about something I cannot forget, and then returning home and, in utter gullibility, being excited about having a message. Chatting with the late night recycler carefully picking through our bin for glass about the balmy weather and the fortification of good attitude even in uncertain times.

In my dream I work in a research lab. Amidst the territorializing of the research for future financial gains, an accidental and fatal contaminant is released. Scientists are left to die, their limbs amputated to supply needed members to those mercurial enough to be still living. While areas of the country are shut down, I visit a bar in Russia with my son. We learn from the local residents that spreading salt on the affected area neutralizes the same contaminant. My son and I return to our local high school evacuation center and I organize a distribution of potato chips.

74

meh \me\ n: mother, used by the baby to label, as when baby sees the birth parent; meh vb: milk, used by the baby when the baby wants to nurse; meh adj: more, used by the baby when the baby wants additional of anything, which, in my mind, is really a compound thought tidily summing up my baby's life: mother-milk-more. Or is it my life?

* * *

Suzanne L. Bunker and Cynthia A. Huff, introducing their edited critique of women's diaries, cite the "braiding" format particular to the way women weave variety in structuring their self-inscriptions. [50] The more elaborate the composite format of the diary, the more the diary begins to reveal the writer's creative communicative process and style via a collage. Jeffery Jenkins, writing in "Cabinet of Curiosity," the introduction to his edited edition of *David Sedaris Diaries: A Visual Compendium*, describes this pieced-

---

[50] Bunkers, Suzanne L. and Cynthia A Huff. "Issues in Studying Women's Diaries: A Theoretical and Critical Introduction." *Inscribing the Daily: Critical Essays on Women's Diaries*, edited by Suzanne L. Bunkers and Cynthia A Huff, University of Massachusetts Press, 1996.

together form of conveying information. "Collage is an integral part of the modern art world's vocabulary and methodology," Jenkins explains, adding that Sedaris "recognizes the intrinsic communicative value of our culture's ceaseless flood of ephemera."[51] Literary techniques may also be applied to the collection of records to break free from the serial, marking-of-time nature of diaries. Lynn Z. Bloom notes the use of foreshadowing, flashbacks, emphasis on a topic rather than a rote daily itemization, and editing and re-writing.[52]

---

[51] Jenkins, Jeffery. "Cabinet of Curiosity." *David Sedaris Diaries: A Visual Compendium*, edited by David Sedaris and Jeffery Jenkins, Little, Brown and Company, 2017.

[52] Bloom, Lynn Z. "'I Write for Myself and Strangers': Private Diaries as Public Documents." *Inscribing the Daily: Critical Essays on Women's Diaries*, edited by Suzanne L. Bunkers and Cynthia Huff, University of Massachusetts Press, 1996, p 29.

75

I dream that I am waiting for a subway with my husband and two sons. The underground train tunnel is characteristically dark and full of silver metal substrate. As I enter the crowded train, my husband and I are separated from my sons. The car, including my husband and all its passengers, takes us to an underground chamber where we are all to be reprimanded for being overbearing. I follow long corridors tiled in brown linoleum that take me out of the subway and into a white clapboard house, neatly furnished and arranged. My husband and I are to live here as penalty.

The house is shared by many adults, all reasonably tempered. As I sit at the dining room table, cleared of dinner food, there is a shelf displaying pictures of my family. I weep copiously. My chest aches in despair over how much I miss my boys. I can see them in real time. They are stooped over their pile of Duplo blocks, assembling constructions, accompanied by the click, click, click of the blocks snapping together. I realize that the boys are absolutely content, and that my circumstance is merely a moment in time for them. They have not and will not notice my absence. In the dining room of the white clapboard house, I am living a parallel life that will always exist only as a moment in time for my boys. I am content in their stability. I continue to grieve nonetheless.

76

Close to bedtime, I stand over my two boys sprawling on the living room couch.

"Boys, get up! I'm about to launch into private adult-oriented activity and you don't want to be around for it. Believe me."

"What? You're gonna watch the news?"

Pushing them into their bedroom, I say "Your room access now includes your bedroom and the bathroom. That's it."

77

Slap. Slap. Slap. Slap.
Flat feet on dry pavement
Quick breathing syncopated to the repetition
Rebellious hot liquors in my blood.[53]
Flecked, fragmented squares of light
where once shadows looked like leaves
Don't trip on the change in luminescence.

---

[53] "Hot and rebellious liquors in my blood." William Shakespeare, *As You Like It*, Act 2, Scene 3, Line 50.

78

Dear Parents,

As part of our Center's dissemination efforts, Patty McGovern, Director and Producer for McGovern and Barr Video Production Co. will be visiting the classroom on Tuesday, February 12th between 10:30 and 1:00 to capture ambient footage of the children in play.

McGovern and Barr Video Production Co. has contracted with the Smithsonian Institute to contribute to an exhibit which will be featured at the Museum, but then will also travel to science centers throughout the country. Footage from our classroom will be part of an exhibit that includes toy artifacts and a video monitor of the children playing.

We are planning for a regular Tuesday as usual. Our circle times will talk about what kinds of play Patty and her camera and sound person might see and hear, and what the equipment will look like. It is our experience that, by preparing the children ahead of time, they are generally acknowledging of a crew's presence but remain occupied with their activities.

The use of a child's first name may occur in the course of recording ambient play, though no first or last names will be used by McGovern and Barr in the production. We will record your child only with your permission. If you agree to have your child recorded, please sign the attached Release Form.

Jane

79

Hallucinations of a Midnight Ring Bearer

The ring bearer's mother attempts a conversational opener over dinner the night following a family wedding. "Well, this is different, not eating with twenty other tables in the room."

The older brother adds, "Yeah, there was so much talking."

A stunned stare abruptly ends the ring bearer's bite, followed by sudden, high-pitched sobbing.

The father calls out in alarm, "What's the matter?"

The older brother attempts to piece together a sequence. "What were you just saying?"

"He's thinking of dinner," the mother explains.

"It's just that I miss the hotel," gulps the ring bearer.

"Ohhhh," launches the father, weaving a tale of a little girl whose parents are African explorers, necessitating her residence in a hotel between the three-year parental stints abroad. The little girl has all her meals in the hotel restaurant and, best of all, gets to use the hotel pool whenever she wants, even when it is closed.

Later that evening, weeping threatens to derail the ring bearer's usual precision drift-off into sleep. He struggles with his utter dejection.

"It's just that I miss my cousins."

"I can't stop crying!"

"It's like I'm in a bad dream."

"I've got a really bad headache."

"I'm cold."

The mother tucks in the ring bearer and wraps her arms around him. The older brother spins in an adjacent desk chair.

"I'm hot."

"My tears are falling on my pillow."

"Why can't we just go back to the hotel?"

"Well, for one reason, this is free and the hotel was eighty-five bucks a night," the mother retorts.

"Can't we get an earlier flight back home, like in the morning?"

"I can't sleep."

That's obvious, the mother silently quips.

"If you just read Harry Potter, I won't think about anything."

"I'm hungry."

It is now two hours after bedtime. The ring bearer drinks a sizable glass of milk, burping out gulped air from his sobs.

"That's the first time I burped right in the middle of drinking."

"You don't have to read anymore," he offers as he slides back into bed. The older brother has given up and moved to the floor.

The ring bearer nestles in his bed, tucking his silk ring-bearer pillow under his chin, rotating it repeatedly as he also clutches his holding blanket. Haltingly he labors, "I . . .I . . .just can't . . . find the . . .words to say how . . .grateful I am for this . . .pillow."

80

Handwritten

Apples from Cobi's for X Country

Pat: Parent Conference

Willie's Object

Homework:
History: Bibliography
1 page summary
Science: Green page
Math: None
Creativity:

English: SSR project

Garden State

PSP Notes
- facial i need carry case
- need memory stick for everything
- UBS cable for internett music
- prices go down in November

Need Lense.com
RADIUS 45

(margin notes)
r
/
but
I

B
day
e's
2 in
ok

us,

?
old
phone

* * *

The white snake in my dream is more than predatory. In its deeply torpid and weighted state it offers the possibility of awakening into feminine wisdom. It holds my puberty, my sexuality, and my capacity for creativity. In its new skin, the white snake has just sloughed off unnecessary pretense for the transformation into the discombobulated world of parenthood. The mother that accompanied my childhood is now me. In motherhood I re-emerge into the vigilance of steering my own children through the wilds of their growth while claiming new initiative for myself. In this I reconnect with Caroline.

There is little diminishment to the startling effects of waking to a sexualized predator. Anyone who grows up identifying as female knows this in her bones. Caroline's mother knew that fear, which is why she protectively cosseted her daughter in clothes revealing little. But the white snake shows me my haunted fear is a sluggish lout. The white snake diary reminds me of the restorative power of healing by embracing life, nurturing new life, and coming full circle to return parental care. The white snake is up and about.

PART IV:
WHITE SNAKE EMERGENT

The notion that the diary is a space for the collection of unencumbered expression, free of judgment, or even, as Woolf used it, a space for free association, is part of the diary's mystique. Diane Ackerman, in writing about the meaning of a collection, calls it "a sort of gallery that ripples through the mind and whose real holdings are the perpetuation of wonder in a maelstrom of social and personal distractions. ... One becomes collected for a spell, gathering up one's curiosities the way rainwater collects."[54] This is the diary as a sought-after place of uninterrupted solace, reverie, reflection, observation, and an assertion of individuality.

Ackerman's rendering of a refuge from the hubbub is quite like the mid-seventeenth-century appearance of a small closet in English homes of wealth and white privilege, where, among other activities, the lady of the house would retire for devotional writing. Effie Botonaki, in her essay "Early Modern Women's Diaries and Closets: 'Chambers of Choice Mercies and Beloved Retirement,'" makes the connection between Christian religious manuals that advised isolation in order to meditate, read, pray and "call to Account the Actions of

---

[54] Ackerman, Diane. *The Zookeeper's Wife: A War Story.* W.W. Norton and Company, 2007, p. 151.

the Day" and the required self-reflective writings, now referred to as women's spiritual diaries.[55] Women sought devotional inscription once, if not more, a day, finding in their diaries a voice at a time when women of privilege were expected to be seen and not heard. "Both the diary and the closet," Botanaki notes, "seek to contain rebellion (i.e., contain thoughts and actions that are designated as immoral) yet...they can potentially enable its emergence and also conceal it by keeping it away from criticism and condemnation."[56] So enclosed, references Botanaki, ecstatic prayer writing sometimes crossed into the erotic.

Journalist Kiyosawa Kiyoshi found protected solace in his World War II diary. Originally writing notes for a history of wartime Japan between 1942 and 1945, Kiyoshi's diary soon became, for him, an act of courageous documentation when criticism of Japanese authoritarianism could mean imprisonment.[57]

Diaries are usually private. Simon Akam, the journalist with a collection of diaries safely stored in his boyhood bedroom, took to rereading this collection.

---

[55] Botanaki, Effie. "Early Modern Women's Diaries and Closets: 'Chambers of Choice Mercies and Beloved Retirement.'" *Recording and Reordering: Essays on the Seventeenth- and Eighteen-Century Diary and Journal,* edited by Dan Doll and Jessica Munns, Bucknell University Press, 2006, pp. 43-64.

[56] Ibid, p. 49.

[57] Kiyosawa, Kiyoshi. *A Diary of Darkness: The Wartime Diary of Kiyosawa Kiyoshi*, edited by Eugene Soviak, translated by Eugene Soviak and Kamiyama Tamie, Princeton University Press, 1999.

Opening these handwritten journals in public places caused a stir: "Reading the diaries in public garnered me strange looks on the London Underground. When a woman inquired I emphasized that that handwriting was my own; I was not perusing another's journal without permission."[58] The diarists of the Renaissance had a special name for this enforced secrecy: libro segreto, a specially designated ledger book of merchant accounts significant to the business and heirs and not to be revealed to outsiders. Safire alerts his readers to the danger of "diary snoops" who fail to recognize that, like a person's mind, the diary is a repository of collected thought protected by the Fourth Amendment against unreasonable search and seizure and the Fifth Amendment protection against self-incrimination. "Just as our home is our castle, our mind is our citadel of privacy—and so should be our mind's most intimate expressions in a personal diary."[59]

---

[58] Akam, Simon. "The Diary Diaries." *The Paris Review,* 10 October, 2013, www.theparisreview.org/blog/2013/10/10/the-diary-diaries/.

[59] Safire, William. "Essay; On Keeping Diaries." *New York Times,* Section A, 18 Aug., 1994, p. 23, www.nytimes.com/1994/08/18/opinion/essay-on-keeping-diaries.html.

81

After sixteen years of marriage and familyhood, much of my perceived angst comes down to time. Life feels too complicated. Both parents work. Two kids are in the throes of puberty, with one who's temporarily lost his mind, several of his textbooks and homework assignments, his keys, and wallet. The other kid is negotiating police actions over possible contraband on the city bus coming home from school and promptly exiting out a broken open rear window. I am leaving myself voicemail messages. Work follows me home. Dinner to make. A husband to listen to.

And I am not even complaining, because I have everything to be grateful for. I have a stimulating and consistent job, with people who appreciate me and treat me well, a loving family, a home with a comforting accumulation of memories, children and a husband who pull their own weight and then some, no commute, I get exercise by riding my bike to work every day. You get the picture.

Yet I struggle with disengagement. Amidst the flurry of contemporary living I have the audacity to be juggling one more ball: boredom. I catch myself after dinner pacing the house. I'm bored. Bored! How could I be? Have I become pubescent as well? Is this what puberty is about? Being so overwhelmed with the juggle of demands that all is abandoned in the flat-line of disengaged boredom?

82

When in distress, can we rely on a benevolent story to guide and soothe our ache and bring us to a place of respite? Mom tells me about Ruth Patterson. Her husband died. Mom was in the post office and the clerk tells her she was startled, astonished in fright, to see Doug Patterson, the deceased, walking out of the post office. Turned out it was Ruth wearing Doug's clothes. Mom says that's what happens on The Island. The wife starts to wear her husband's clothes. Does Ruth feel respite in Doug's shirt, pants, coat, hat? What is Ruth's story now? Can she feel Doug in his clothes?

My story tonight starts several weeks ago when I became aware of an undefined disjointed quality. That night I dream that my cousin calls, waking me. My cousin rarely calls me. I rarely call him. Three hours' time difference, juggling the immediacy of family. As he begins to talk, my other cousin, his brother, speaks, and I realize they have organized a conference call. I am thoroughly impressed that they have done this for me. They are calling to tell me that I am OK.

I am so touched by their call that I wake up for real and discover I have a bad headache. Now I am really happy my cousins called and woke me because I can pop a couple of aspirin and go back to bed and hopefully wake up more refreshed than if I had not taken aspirin.

In the morning I tell everyone I see. I tell my husband. I tell my two kids. I tell my co-workers: "I got a conference call from my cousins last night. They called to tell me I was OK! It was a dream, but it was so sweet." Everyone heard about my conference call.

I have been plagued by revealing demeanor all my life. I try and keep my feelings private (even to myself?). Inevitably someone will notice. "Is there something wrong?" What are they seeing? A furrowed brow? A disengaged gaze? Can people sense less-than-vibrant energy or, more accurately, diffuse energy? Why not?

I open the door to our administrative wing and remember an event tomorrow and the receptionist says, "I was just thinking of you and reminding myself to tell you about—" of course, the very same event. If we can so easily share mental correspondence, why not also pick up on another's state of mind or spirit?

I ask for three vacation days. My disjointed feelings have escalated to distress. On my vacation request form I write in the comment box: "I am feeling a little impatient with the kids and three days off would help me re-settle." In the dark hour before dawn the following morning, I get a real call from my cousin.

He tells me Dad is dead. He died in his sleep.

I can't help feeling that the startled shock of that call was somehow tempered by recognizing that I needed to take care of myself. That, and the confirmation of my cousins' love and care for me from their conference call.

* * *

Selectivity lurks for all diarists. Self-imposed censorship feels only smart. "Early on," Sedaris explains in a 2017 interview with the AV Club, "you had to write in a book. That is why I never wrote about sex. You had to worry that someone was going to find your diary."[60] Helen Garner was so guarded about her writing that before leaving for university, she burned all her diaries in the backyard. "I just tore them up and dropped them into this fiery furnace and my mother was standing there saying, Please let me read them. Please let me read just one page? And I said, Absolutely not."[61] Lozano, the pocket-sized diarist, returned to her notebooks for publication, editing the entries and sometimes blacking out entire pages. She retained the original "PRIVATE" firmly written in black marker on the covers. Did Pepys write in shorthand as a guard against unwanted intruders?

Safire's call to arms came after the Packwood v. Senate Select Committee on Ethics Supreme Court ruling making any documentation penned by a public servant open to scrutiny. Citing diarist Joshua Steiner, Safire underscores the fear shadowing what might no longer be private: "Been battling w/ the RTC/Madison. Wrote two pages about what's been going on, suddenly realized that I could be subpoenaed like Packwood and

---

[60] Sedaris, David. "David Sedaris on his new book of old diaries plus a few shit stories," interviewed by Caitlin Penzymoog, *AVClub, 30* May, 2017, 12:00 a.m., www.avclub.com/david-sedaris-on-his-new-book-of-old-diaries-plus-a-fe-1798262446 .

[61] Garner, Helen. "Helen Garner on Court Burning Diaries and the Violence of Love: John Freeman in Conversation with the Author of *Everywhere I Look*," interviewed by John Freeman, *Literary Hub*, 27 September, 2016. lithub.com/helen-garner-on-court-burning-diaries-and-the-violence-of-love/.

the most innocuous comments could be taken out of context. So on that subject, nothing."[62] Nin does not mention in any of her diaries that she had two husbands simultaneously, one on each coast, purportedly so she could maintain her partners' financial support for her art.

In Sedaris' introduction to *Theft by Finding: Diaries 1977–2002*, he notes the significant themes left out of his entries. In his case, selectivity is more about what he is prepared to reveal. "You'd think I'd have addressed my drinking, at least in the privacy of my diary, but it's rarely mentioned. To type that word—alcoholic—would have made it real, so I never recounted the talking-to's I got from Hugh and certain helpful people in my family. Similarly, it took me a while...to write the word gay. 'Oh, please,' I said out loud to my twenty-year-old self while reading my earliest diaries. 'Who do you think you're kidding?'"[63]

With the advent of digital media, some feel more protected. Sedaris locks his digital diary files. Other diarists write on private Twitter accounts. Blogger

---

[62] Safire, William. "Essay; On Keeping Diaries." *New York Times,* Section A, 18 Aug., 1994, p. 23, www.nytimes.com/1994/08/18/opinion/essay-on-keeping-diaries.html.

[63] Sedaris, David. *Theft by Finding: Diaries 1977-2002.* Little Brown and Company, 2017, p. 7.

Magnanti of Belle du Jour fame came clean in November of 2009 after six years of anonymity (even her agent was unaware of her name), saying in *The Guardian* interview, "It feels so much better on this side. Not to have to tell lies, hide things from the people I care about."[64]

---

[64] Gallagher, Paul and Peter Walker. "Belle du Jour Blogger Unmasks Herself as 'Big-Mouthed Boyfriend' Looms." *The Guardian, 15* November, 2009. www.theguardian.com/technology/2009/nov/15/belle-de-jour-author-blogger-brooke-magnanti.

83

I have become the kind of person I am used to tolerating with a generous spirit.

Where I used to travel uncharted territory by
thumb
      train
         motorcycle
           bus

Regularly reminded and thrilled by the power of serendipity,

I now travel the uncharted grounds of my own routinized life

Again relying on what seems unabashedly like serendipity when I remarkably find my way to

a meeting place I have already been to
          a finished piece of writing in the pile of recycling

Do I assume I am a wasteland of potential or can I recognize the depth of water I choose to swim in?

84

Why the surge of productivity just now after several days of unscrupulously rash banishments of initiative? Was it the Mennonite family holiday greeting? "Father continues to compose hymns during his long commute. Mother keeps bread on the table, sourdough recently, and has taken up mitten knitting in the evenings. I continue to work in the accounting office and fill my spare hours with writing, drawing, and dishwashing." Obviously my aspirations are amiss. I may not excel at sourdough, but I scour the refrigerator for old vegetables and cooked leftovers for stir fried rice. I boil potatoes for tomorrow morning's home fries.

A doctor on the radio reports that the same pleasurable rush of endorphins we love so much when exercising aerobically is also found when we learn something new. That night I dream my investigation is going awry. Each new lead inexplicably dissolves in an evaporation of clues. Witnesses scurry away just as I arrive. I suspect an inside informant. I voice my concerns to my fellow detectives, resulting in a wrestling match with my superior as he attempts to dispose of pertinent files.

Two witnesses in the investigation are now vulnerable to retribution. Their lives are in danger.

In alarm, I seek them out and find them home, blissfully unaware. If I can so easily locate them, certainly the bad detective will find them. But the couple remains calm, ignoring my pre-emptive pleas to flee. The bad detective stalks close by. The couple and I crouch out of sight. We are dead ducks.

There is a scuffle. My oldest son is in the house. He and I are in hand-to-hand combat. I am fighting my son to save this couple's life. I bend my son's arm joint out of its socket. This does not deter him. He feels no pain. Oedipus killed his father—albeit to assert his independence with his mother—but nonetheless, my son's flight from the nest appears to include my demise. The tug and pull of pubescent selfhood is an unnerving counterpoint to my own self-assessment.

85

"You have an eye for fashion, Mom, right?"

"Right."

"So could I get your opinion on a dress?"

"Sure."

I reach for my satchel. "How about I pop into your bathroom and change, so you can see the dress, OK?"

"OK."

"OK. I am going to change in your bathroom. I will be right out in a minute, all right?"

"All right."

Six days ago I received a call from my cousin. Mom had a stroke and was in rehab. I knew the routine: pack light, sleep at my cousin's, and carry a satchel stocked with activities to offer Mom. At the last minute, I thought about my designer cocktail dress made in a malleable, metal-threaded fabric. Mom would love to see this dress, which conveniently can be wadded up in a satchel without wrinkling.

I slide my jeans off over the high heeled Mary Jane's I have worn all week for just this moment, pull off my top and step into the dress. My heart beats fast as I zip up from behind. I know full well I must try and temper my excitement. This is my fantasy, which I have learned may not conform to any immediate moment in Mom's state of mind. Still, it is a cool fantasy. As promised, I have dressed in a minute.

I pop out from the bathroom, arms outstretched, face beaming, and Mom's reaction is everything I could have hoped for.

"Oh! Wonderful!" my mother gasps. "Wonderful!"

"You like it?"

"Oh, yes!"

I turn slowly.

"Oh! Lovely!"

"So, you think this dress works?"

"Yes, it does."

"You think this is an OK dress for me?"

"Oh, yes!"

Mom and I spend the next three quarters of an hour going over every aspect of the dress: How does it look when part of the shoulder is tufted up? Better down? Let's look at it up again. Okay, what about the other shoulder? What about both together? Should they both be up? Both down? Only one down? What does Mom think about the exposed back? What about the flaring skirt? Should we go with an exposed leg? No? In finale, I bring out a necklace, and together Mom and I discuss how the dress works with and without the necklace.

Like so many points in this six-day visit, there comes a time of pause. A time of rest. I find these times peaceful. No agenda. Just this moment. Together. I understand Mom's pace at this point in her life. Some of the time she is content to just be. I am grateful to be with her. Mom in her wheelchair. Me standing in front. Quiet.

The hours in the rehab nursing home drag for me, however. This fun with the dress has been a great time kill. After several minutes pass, I begin to think: Gee, Mom does have dementia. I wonder if we can do this again?

"Mom? ... Mom?"

"Yes?"

"I need to use the bathroom, OK?"

"Sure."

"OK. I'm going to use your bathroom. I will be right out, all right?"

"All right."

I retreat and shut the door. I wait. And wait. I wait some more. I wait even more. I smile. For good measure, I wait still more.

Then I pop out, arms outstretched, face beaming towards my mom.

"Jane," Mom says with a weary and familiar exasperation, "you're going to have to stay in there longer."

86

What the Teacher Researcher Does
Jane Perry

- Elaborates on children's interest and curiosity by creating physical places for play and exploration
- Recognizes attempts by children to experiment
- Recognizes children's extensions of projects
- Asks for clarification and information from children
- Nurtures children's developing expertise
- Suggests new ideas to elaborate on children's interactions
- Asks questions to encourage articulation of children's points of view
- Recognizes children's desire to experience mastery
- Supports children's feelings of accomplishment and expertise
- Collects observations of children to answer questions and anticipate next steps
- Shares information with families, colleagues, and the public

* * *

Censorship can be imposed from the outside. Kiyoshi knew full well the danger he was in by maintaining his diary for a historical record but he continued. Pepys no doubt penned his seventeenth-century accounts with posterity in mind, yet his emboldened aggression toward women includes destroying his wife Bess' diary, with, as Judy Simons notes in her essay "Invented Lives: Textuality and Power in Early Women's Diaries," "an uneasy combination of pride and guilt."[65] Simons includes the brutal Pepys incident:

> 9 January (1663) I was vexed at it and desired her and then commanded her to teare it – which she desired to be excused it; I forced it from her and tore it, and withal took her other bundle of papers from her and leapt out of bed and in my shirt clapped them into the pockets of my breeches that she might not get them from me; and having got on my stockings and breeches and gown, I pulled them out one by one and tore them all before her face, though it went against my heart to do it, she crying and desiring me not to do it.[66]

---

[65] Simons, Judy. "Invented Lives: Textuality and Power in Early Women's Diaries." *Inscribing the Daily: Critical Essays on Women's Diaries,* edited by Suzanne L. Bunkers and Cynthia A Huff, University of Massachusetts Press, 1996, pp. 252-263.

[66] Ibid, p. 252.

Percy Shelley, reports Harriet Blodgett in *Centuries of Female Days: Englishwomen's Private Diaries*, assumed ghost authorship for his wife, not an uncommon practice at the time, says Blodgett, during indisposed circumstances as in the birth of a child.[67] Charles Lutwidge Dodson, writing as Lewis Carroll, was a diarist. Several years of his diary collection, along with visibly removed pages from those released for archive purposes, have been removed, most likely by family, to hide personal information pertaining to Dodson's infatuation with eleven-year-old Alice Lidell.

Does the diary offer a portrait of the diarist? We read diaries to see the world through the eyes of the author, to notice what they find interesting and what they ruminate upon. Sometimes the diary can show us a glimpse of a different time, or place or social circle. But the diary is always a filtered collection. That we are reading a diary at all is open to at least an ethical consideration. Safire asks that we be highly cautious of "the rush to break the seal of the self-confessional."[68]

---

[67] Blodgett, Harriet. *Centuries of Female Days: Englishwomen's Private Diaries*, Rutgers University Press, 1988.

[68] Safire, William. "Essay; On Keeping Diaries." *New York Times,* Section A, 18 Aug., 1994, p. 23, www.nytimes.com/1994/08/18/opinion/essay-on-keeping-diaries.html.

87

Do you want to say goodbye?

       You want to get focused
       on yourself?

Yes.

       Yes.

It was good to talk with you today.
I am happy.

       Yes. I feel the same way.

I am happy. May I call you again?

       You will call again?

Yes.
Can you say goodbye for now?

       I can't. Wait a minute.

I love you, Mom.

       Laughs. Yeah.
       I know you do.

I will call again.

       Yes. I'd like you to do that.
       I don't know the different flin.
       Flin.
       I don't know if it.
       I don't know if it's working.

I know it will.

       It's good you *know* it will. Yes.
       The telephone.

Shall we say goodbye?
I love you so much.

                              I love *you* so much.
Thank you for loving me.
                              You don't know?
I like it when you say it.
I love you.

                              Well, I think I love you.
                              Laughs.
                              I don't know.
                              It.
I am going to say goodbye and I will call again.
I feel very tender because I love you so much.
Are you going to say bye now?
                              Yes.
                              Okay, that makes sense.
Bye.

                              Bye bye.

88

Dear Caroline,

How great to get your email. I am posting this because in a rash rush prompted by an all too familiar Let-Me-Clean-So-I-Can-Manage-Emotions-I-Am-Trying-Not-To-Feel-Too-Deeply, I purged literally 4,200 Inbox emails and lost yours. So I am touched by your tenacity.

I am so sorry to hear about your father. I am heartened that he got to honor his choices until the end. That is a solace.

So, you are a parent of a middle schooler!

Middle school, where at dinner one night my boys announced, after being at Gay Alliance after school, that their friend Ricky had decided to go back in the closet. Maybe I love middle school so much because it is a lot like the preschool years: amazing growth requiring acclimating to their bodies all over again, voice modulation, playing with identities, vivid peer dynamics. Your son has amazing glow, and I only know him from the still Best Seasonal Card Award. We do not know then that in those hormone-fueled years our parental vigilance can surface later in companionable twenty-something-year-olds.

I understand your immediate refocus on your mother after your dad died. A different kind of partnership in foreign territory, perhaps. Thank you for confiding so I can send you my love.

My mom died in January of this year, in comfort and peace with hospice care at her home. A story for another time, as you say, but I am eternally grateful for the inspired connection my mom and I were able to maintain alongside her dementia. It was all about singing. Singing to her and reassuring her that I was well, her family was well, and we were all together.

And life goes on. Our oldest is living with us. I told him yesterday that I had been remembering when he was a kid and could not stop sucking his thumb. The roof of his mouth was reshaping. We had the orthodontist re-stretch his mouth and attach a cage-like grill to block his thumb. I said I wondered if Dad and I would need to put a cage on the front door to keep him out of the house. . . pssst . . . I will miss him when he moves out.

Our other son called all in a dither. He got a job offer but it is on commission only, which puts him back to square one in terms of post-graduation employment if he follows his head and gut and declines this offer. I told him he was doing better than me, when I graduated and earned money under the table as a model for the art department. Remember that? "That was you?!" he yelped. He had just come from his art class and had worked for the first time in his life with a live model. "She was so relaxed," he observed.

Lots and lots of love to you.

Take care,

Jane

89

If you spend a lot of time thinking how old you are
You
Put away
Many days
So you don't
Have the
Days to think about.

(The author's mother, Anne G. Perry, in 36 seconds,
on the practicalities involved when aging.)

* * *

To whom is the diarist writing? Bloom, using a
Gertrude Stein quote, calls out "the audience hovering
at the edge of the page" that "facilitates the work's
ultimate focus, providing the impetus either for the
initial writing or for transforming what might have
been casual, fragmented jottings into a more carefully
crafted, contextually coherent work."[69] Some diaries
are written for family or historical posterity. Women's

---

[69] Bloom, Lynn Z. "'I Write for Myself and Strangers': Private
Diaries as Public Documents." *Inscribing the Daily: Critical Essays
on Women's Diaries*, edited by Suzanne L. Bunkers and Cynthia
Huff, University of Massachusetts Press, 1996, p. 23.

spiritual diaries were written to God. Garner's editorial filter toward the audience is incendiary. So enamored with her first diary burning, she repeated it, telling the story to *LitHub*: "I thought, *Oh, perhaps I should have a look at these books and see if they're worth keeping*. And they were just so terrible, all the ones up to about 1980. There were just whingy, that sort of girl's whingy, *He doesn't love me, what have I done wrong? I know it must be my fault*. And all that sort of crap. So I just made another fire in the backyard."[70] Yet even she, knowing full well that she is capable of incineration, writes with a "fantasized reader" in mind.[71]

Some diaries are contested. The diary of Jack The Ripper, whose author was believed to be James Maybrick (1838–1889) was unearthed in 1992 by a former scrap-metal dealer in Liverpool who purportedly found it in his attic, or his friend's attic. The diary has undergone several forensic analyses, including scanning electron microscopy, a link to a Liverpool Art shop in operation in the 1940s as the only known supplier of the chemically-identified diary ink, an analysis of the preservative compound in the ink that dates to 1974, to a final conclusion in 2015 that the diary

---

[70] Garner, Helen. "Helen Garner on Court Burning Diaries and the Violence of Love: John Freeman in Conversation with the Author of *Everywhere I Look*," interviewed by John Freeman, *Literary Hub*, 27 September, 2016. lithub.com/helen-garner-on-court-burning-diaries-and-the-violence-of-love/.

[71] Ibid.

was a modern hoax—until an English film director, actor, novelist and screenwriter claimed to have new forensics of authenticity.[72]

---

[72] Robinson, Bruce B. *They All Love Jack: Busting the Ripper.* Harper, 2015.

90

I receive a neuropsychological report as part of legal proceedings after a head-on collision with a car while doing errands on my bicycle. This is a page from that report.

PERSONALITY FUNCTIONING

Results from Minnesota Multiphasic Personality Inventory-2 (MMPI-2)

It should be noted that this test was scored and interpreted with the aid of a computer program provided by the test distributor. The following is a summary of the test results from the computer program.

The test results indicated that there were some concerns regarding the validity findings inasmuch as Ms. Perry endorsed responses so as to present herself in an overly positive light. She tended to minimize faults and deny psychological problems. As a result, the clinical profile may underestimate her problems.

Individuals with similar test results tend to be somewhat rigid and inflexible in their approach to problems and may not be open to psychological self-evaluation. She may project an excessively positive self-image.

All of Ms. Perry's clinical scales were well within normal limits. The current clinical findings indicate that she tends to be optimistic. She tends to stress the positive side of life. She may tend to deny or ignore problems at times. She may tend to view other people and herself in an overly positive fashion.

The results also indicate that she has an average interest in being with other people and is not socially isolated or withdrawn. She meets and interacts with other people with relative ease.

Her scores on the content scales indicate that she tries to project a positive attitude about life and interpersonal relationships with an open and accepting attitude. She views her home life as positive. She reports that it is pleasant and problem free. She feels she has a great deal of emotional support from those around her.

Inasmuch as her clinical profile is within normal limits, no diagnoses are suggested.

Results from the Personality Assessment Inventory (PAI)

It should be noted that the PAI was scored and interpreted with the aid of a computer program provided by the test distributor. The following is a summary of the results from the computerized interpretation.

The validity findings indicated that Ms. Perry tended to portray herself as being relatively free of common shortcomings to which most individuals will admit. She may be reluctant to accept minor faults in herself. Given her tendency to repress undesirable characteristics, the clinical results should be considered with caution. While there is no evidence that she intentionally tried to distort the profile, the results may under represent the extent of her problems.

91

#WhyIDidntReport I can't even tell myself yet.

8:44 AM - 22 Sep 2018

1 Retweet **2** Likes

1 2

92

Eight eggs cracked into the bowl after resting for twenty minutes on the counter. The egg beater makes Caroline taste metal. Something about the dander sloughing off the old prongs. Who used this beater before her? Caroline found it in an airless, stuffy kitchen at an estate sale. It looked like someone had emptied a kitchen drawer on the table. Was its owner white haired now, sloughing off her own dander? Did she bring the back of her hand to her forehead to wipe away a wisp of hair? The windows have sheer yellow curtains, with eyelets. The windows are open, because the birds are singing into the kitchen. A cicada buzzes away all memory.

The prongs of the egg beater whir as Caroline cranks the rotating gear until she notices she is out of breath. What she has not noticed until just now is a muffled cadenced call coming from the area of her feet. She turns her head to locate the sound, bending to follow its direction. In a moment of recognition, then immediate panic, she hears her young granddaughter, and unlatches the white enamel cupboard in which she had been playing.

*   *   *

What the diarist composes and why, and to whom, and in what form, and then whether the public sees it, all make up what diary is. Bloom, quoting Woolf, who embraced a loose, composite format in her diaries, nonetheless sought a standard of literary polish: "I should like to come back, after a year or two, & find that the collection had sorted itself & refined itself & coalesced, as such deposits so mysteriously do, into mould, transparent enough to reflect the light of our life, & yet steady, tranquil composed with the aloofness of a work of art."[73]

One thing a diary is not, is an offer of an ending. Diary entries eventually and simply stop. The diarist has died, or is too weak to continue, or worries about impending blindness, or the venture is complete, or circumstances change, or the ink stays frozen, or the diarist moves on to other habits. For Dan Doll and Jessica Munns, the diary "is, and perhaps always will

---

[73] Bloom, Lynn Z. "'I Write for Myself and Strangers': Private Diaries as Public Documents." *Inscribing the Daily: Critical Essays on Women's Diaries*, edited by Suzanne L. Bunkers and Cynthia Huff, University of Massachusetts Press, 1996, p 29.

remain, a liminal form that disturbs our sense of what is 'real' and what is 'fiction'."[74]

---

[74] Doll, Dan and Jessica Munns. "Introduction." *Recording and Reordering: Essays on the Seventeenth- and Eighteenth-Century Diary and Journal*, edited by Dan Doll and Jessica Munns, Bucknell University Press, 2006, p. 20.

93

 First Parish in Concord, *Concord, Massachusetts*
GATHERED 1636

Dear Mr. and Mrs. Perry,

Each year at this time the Church School sends reports to parents concerning the progress of their children. It has been a pleasure to have Jane in my class with her pleasant smile.

She is always eager to participate in our activities. At times she becomes too excited and then becomes noisy. I believe this is because of her eagerness to take part in our activities.

Jane does good hand work. As Jane becomes used to the idea of new things happening I am sure she will become more calm. Her eagerness should not be stopped.

Sincerely yours,
Ruth Ames

I laid my face against my arm, and there
It stayed for the length of time it takes two swarms
Of bees to carry a snake through a wide garden,
Past a sleeping swan, past the dead roses nailed
To the wall, past the small pond. And when
I looked up the bees and the snake were gone,
But the garden smelled of broken fruit, and across
The grass a shadow lay for which there was no source,
A narrow plinth dividing the garden, and the air
Was like the air after a fire, or before a storm,
Ungodly still, but full of dark shapes turning. [75]

[75] Kelly, Brigit Pegeen. "The Dragon." *New England Review*, 2002, Volume 23.2, p. 8, www.nereview.com/vol-35-no-3-2014/brigit-pegeen-kelly/.

ACKNOWLEDGMENTS

I want to thank Nick Courtright at Atmosphere Press for embracing this genre-bending, multi-genre, multi-media project and to everyone at Atmosphere Press for shepherding White Snake Diary into existence. Thank you to Kyle McCord for his excellent editorial expertise and to Erin Cosyn for crisp and meticulous proofreading. Thank you to Cameron Finch for remarkable artistry in interior design. I am so grateful to Atmosphere Press for an invigorating and gratifying creative partnership.

Thank you to Amber Lea Starfire and Christine Steers for their invaluable editorial support that improved this book mightily. Thank you to Bob Devaney for illustration technical support. Thank you to Bruce Perry for copy proofing. I want to thank several people for graciously reading early drafts of this project, including Ai'fe Murray, Renata Ewing, Sari Broner, Patrick Devaney, Mary E. Hutchison, and Michelle Sherry. Thank you to Joan Schwartz for title suggestion. Thank you to Patrick and William Devaney for the use of their school assignments.

ABOUT ATMOSPHERE PRESS

Atmosphere Press is an independent, full-service publisher for excellent books in all genres and for all audiences. Learn more about what we do at atmospherepress.com.

We encourage you to check out some of Atmosphere's latest releases, which are available at Amazon.com and via order from your local bookstore:

Rags to Rags, nonfiction by Ellie Guzman
Heat in the Vegas Night, nonfiction by Jerry Reedy
Evelio's Garden, nonfiction by Sandra Shaw Homer
Difficulty Swallowing, essays by Kym Cunningham
A User Guide to the Unconscious Mind, nonfiction by Tatiana Lukyanova
To the Next Step: Your Guide from High School and College to The Real World, nonfiction by Kyle Grappone
Breathing New Life: Finding Happiness after Tragedy, nonfiction by Bunny Leach
Love Your Vibe: Using the Power of Sound to Take Command of Your Life, nonfiction by Matt Omo
Transcendence, poetry and images by Vincent Bahar Towliat
Letting Nicki Go: A Mother's Journey through Her Daughter's Cancer, nonfiction by Bunny Leach

ABOUT THE AUTHOR

Jane P. Perry uses voices and ephemera to tell stories. She is an expert in outdoor play, and has written on the import- ance of play in early childhood, Occupy Oak- land, and familyhood. She also tells stories with sound art, where the auditory sense provides a rich channel of imagination. Jane is a retired teacher and re- searcher with the University of California, Berkeley Harold E. Jones Child Study Center. She lives in the territory of Huichin on unceded land of the Chochenyo Ohlone (Oakland). Proceeds from the sale of this book go to The Sogorea Te Land Trust, an urban Indigenous women-led 501c3 organization facilitating the return of SF Bay land to Indigenous stewardship, healing from the legacies of colonization and genocide, promotion of a different way of living, and the continuation of the work that the ancestors and future generations call us to do. For more information on Jane P. Perry go to janepperry.com.